Tax Planning For The Family Home

How to avoid CGT, Income Tax & Inheritance Tax on Private Residences

Lee J Hadnum

IMPORTANT LEGAL NOTICES:

DISCLAIMER

CONTENTS

ABOUT THE AUTHOR

Lee Hadnum LLB ACA CTA is an international tax specialist. He is a Chartered Accountant and Chartered Tax Adviser and is the Editor of the popular tax planning website:

www.wealthprotectionreport.co.uk

Lee is also the author of a number of best selling tax planning books including:

- **Tax Planning Techniques Of The Rich & Famous** - Essential reading for anyone who wants to use the same tax planning techniques as the most successful Entrepreneurs, large corporations and celebrities

- **The Worlds Best Tax Havens 2014/2015**– 230 page book looking at the worlds best offshore jurisdictions in detail

- **Non Resident & Offshore Tax Planning 2014/2015**– Offshore tax planning for UK residents or anyone looking to purchase UK property or trade in the UK. A comprehensive guide.

- **Tax Planning With Offshore Companies & Trusts: The A-Z Guide** - Detailed analysis of when and how you can use offshore companies and trusts to reduce your UK taxes

- **Tax Planning For Company Owners** – How company owners can reduce income tax, corporation tax and NICs

- **How To Avoid CGT In 2013/2014** – Tax planning for anyone looking to reduce UK capital gains tax

- **Buy To Let Tax Planning** – How property investors can reduce income tax, CGT and inheritance tax

- **Asset Protection Handbook** – Looks at strategies to ringfence your assets in today's increasing litigious climate

- **Working Overseas Guide** – Comprehensive analysis of how you can save tax when working overseas

- **Double Tax Treaty Planning** – How you can use double tax treaties to reduce UK taxes

CHAPTER 1

SELLING YOUR MAIN RESIDENCE – HOW CAPITAL GAINS TAX APPLIES

Selling property of any kind is subject to capital gains tax ("CGT").

Although many accountants would have you believe otherwise, the basic capital gains tax calculation is pretty straightforward.

Once you sell property you have what are called 'disposal proceeds'. Subtracting the purchase cost of the property you end up with what most people would describe as their profit.

However, this is not the amount that gets taxed. From your profit you can deduct certain expenses, such as stamp duty and agency/solicitors fees.

There is then the potential to offset some reliefs depending on the property in question and the circumstances of the disposal. It may be that after offsetting these reliefs there is no CGT to pay.

On the other hand even though a property has been occupied as your main residence, there could be some CGT to pay.

After you've deducted your reliefs you can deduct your annual capital gains tax exemption. Whatever's left gets taxed at either 18% or 28%.

A typical capital gains tax calculation is summarised in Table 1.

Table 1: Typical CGT Calculation

Proceeds   X

Less:
Acquisition cost   (X)

Deductible expenses	(X)
Reliefs	(X)
Chargeable gain	X
Less:	
Annual exemption	(X)
Taxable gain	X

Example

Pat sells a share in a property for £16,000. He bought it for £4,000. His profit is therefore £12,000. From this we subtract deductible expenditure of, say, £75 (representing stamp duty and broker's commission).

He can offset the annual CGT exemption of £11,000 and deducting this leaves a taxable gain of £925. If he is a basic-rate taxpayer he'll then pay CGT at 18%, producing a tax bill of £166.50.

Of course, matters aren't always this simple. Every step of the typical CGT calculation outlined above has a variety of 'ifs', 'buts' and 'maybes'.

The CGT Rate

Capital gains are taxed at either 18% (basic-rate taxpayers) or 28% (higher-rate taxpayers), or maybe a combination of both, depending on how much income you earn and the size of your capital gains.

If you have no other income (or it is covered by your income tax personal allowance) then the first £31,865 of your capital gains is taxed at 18%. £31,865 is the basic-rate tax band for the 2014/15 tax year.

If you have income which completely uses up your basic-rate tax band you will pay 28% tax on your capital gains.

If your income is within the basic-rate tax band, you can use the remainder for capital gains tax purposes, which means you will pay 18% CGT on some or all of your gains. Any gains in excess of the basic-rate band will be taxed at 28%.

Example

Patrick sold a property in July 2014. He realised a capital gain of £50,000 after deducting his annual CGT exemption.

He has taxable income of £20,000 for the 2014/15 tax year, after deducting his income tax personal allowance.

The basic-rate band is £31,865 for 2014/15. Of this £20,000 is used up by Patrick's income, leaving £11,865 for capital gains tax purposes.

His £50,000 capital gain will therefore be taxed as follows:

£11,865 @ 18%   £2,136

£38,135 @ 28%   £10,687

Total   £12,823

The effective rate of CGT for Patrick is therefore 25% (£12,823/£50,000) and is a mixture of the 18% and 28% tax rates.

Note that if you have no other income, your income tax personal allowance CANNOT be offset against your taxable capital gains.

For example, if your spouse earns no income but realises a capital gain that is £1,000 more than the annual CGT exemption, this will be fully taxed at 18% or 28%.

Example

In the 2014/15 tax year, Fred earns a salary of £28,000 and has taxable gains of £12,500 from a property. His annual exemption is already utilised. His tax calculation is as follows:

	Salary	£28,000
Less:	Personal allowance	-£10,000
		£18,000

Tax on salary:

18,000 @ 20%	£3,600
Income tax	£3,600

Next we calculate Steven's capital gains tax liability:

Tax on property disposal:

£12,500 @ 18%	£2,250
Total CGT	£2,250

The capital gain of £12,500 will be taxed at 18% because it is fully covered by Fred's remaining basic-rate tax band.

Effective CGT Rates

Although the maximum tax rate is now 28%, when you take into account the annual CGT exemption, which protects a further £11,000 per person, and other deductions, your 'effective tax rate' will often be much lower than 28%.

By 'effective tax rate' we mean the total tax expressed as a percentage of your profits.

You only pay 28% on your 'chargeable gains' and your chargeable gains are often much lower than your actual profits.

What are Your Proceeds?

In the vast majority of cases the disposal proceeds are simply the cash received when the property is sold.

However, if you sell your property to a 'connected person' for less than it's worth or if the transaction is not at 'arm's length', the disposal proceeds will be the true market value of the property, rather than the payment you receive (which may be significantly less).

Connected persons include:

- Your spouse
- Your children or remoter descendants
- Your parents or remoter ancestors
- Your brothers and sisters and their spouses
- Your spouse's relatives, eg brothers, sisters or parents.
- Business partners Although your husband or wife is a connected person, it's critical to point out that there is no capital gains tax payable if you transfer assets to your spouse or civil partner.

Example

Peter decides to transfer a property to his brother. The market value of the property is £75,000. The gift will represent a disposal by Peter and capital gains tax will be payable, based on proceeds of £75,000

There are other situations where the transaction might not be at arm's length and market value will be substituted for the actual disposal proceeds, for example transfers between unmarried couples.

In these circumstances the onus of proof that the transaction was not at arm's length rests with Revenue and Customs.

What is Your Acquisition Cost?

In most cases the cost of property will be the amount you paid for it.

If the property was transferred to you at less than market value (as in the example above) your base cost will be the market value of the property.

If you bought the property prior to 31 March 1982, the so-called MV82 rule comes into play. In these circumstances, the acquisition cost is deemed to be the value of the property on 31 March 1982. This provision effectively eliminates tax on any profit earned before 31 March 1982.

Deductible Expenses

Once you've subtracted the acquisition cost from the disposal proceeds, you can claim costs directly related to the acquisition and disposal of the property.

By and large, the main costs you can claim are:

- Stamp duty
- Agency fees
- Legal fees on buying and selling

As well as these "incidental expenses" you can also deduct "Enhancement Expenditure". These are costs that you incur on improving the property (eg a new kitchen, bathroom etc). The main caveat here is that the cost needs to be reflected in the "State and Nature" of the property at the date of disposal.

Therefore if you have incurred expenditure on a new kitchen which is subsequently removed prior to sale, the costs wouldn't be allowed as "Enhancement Expenditure".

How to reduce CGT on disposal?

We've looked at how CGT is calculated above. However, in most cases the disposal of your main residence will be completely free of CGT.

This is because of Principal Private Residence relief which will provide a full or partial CGT exemption where a property has been occupied as a main residence.

In the next chapter we look at when a property can be a main residence for CGT purposes.

CHAPTER 2

ESTABLISHING A PROPERTY AS A MAIN RESIDENCE IN 2014

Principal Private residence ('PPR') relief exempts a proportion of the gain on a property, when the property disposed of has been the owners main residence.

Therefore to qualify for this relief two conditions need to be satisfied:

- the property must be occupied as a residence, and
- it must be the main residence

In order to be a residence you need to own an interest in the property. This can be either a freehold or leasehold interest - but not a licence to occupy.

Of key importance to many is how long it is necessary to occupy a property for before it can qualify as a residence/main residence.

Residence is not defined in the legislation, however the Revenue expect a degree of permanence, therefore occupation for only a handful of days each year would not constitute residence. Whilst drawn from a different context (in connection with the availability of mortgage interest relief) a Revenue extra statutory concession suggested that a period of occupation of not less than three months was required to establish a property as the only or main residence.

Whilst the MIRAS position is influential it is not conclusive.

There are no hard and fast rules as to how long to occupy the property before it can be classed as a residence. Some commentators suggest occupying a property for a period of 12 months, although there is no fixed period set by the Revenue and they frequently refer to the 'quality' as opposed to the 'quantity'of the occupation. It is important to ensure that the residence is genuine. For example the property should be your registered address for the electoral register, and your employers should be informed of the new address

It's a matter of fact when a property is a residence, and a tax inspector will look at the whole circumstances surrounding the occupation of the property. The checklist below highlights some of the key factual issues to consider.

Evidence to make a property a main residence

Yes	No	Evidence
		Was the mortgage obtained on the basis of the property being the main residence?
		Is the Property a freehold property?
		Are the utility bills etc addressed to you?
		Was there continuous and regular occupation of the property by you?
		Was the house the family home?
		Did your tax return/Revenue correspondence go to this property?
		Did letters from your employer go to this property?
		Did you work close to this property?
		Are any bills for work etc billed to this property?

Is the property registered as your main residence with the local authority?

Was this property furnished with your furniture

Recent Developments

Of course for most people this won't even be an issue. They will own one property and this will be the main residence. What if they own two or more properties though? Well this is when you'd need to look at the matters as highlighted above to try and see which of the properties was the main residence.

If you've got a property that is let and you're looking to reduce the capital gains tax charge on the future disposal a popular option is to consider occupying it as a main residence.

In this case it would then qualify for at least partial principal private residence ('PPR') relief as well as lettings relief.

If this applies to you you'd again need to consider the above and actually make sure it was your home for a suitable period (say 6-12 months +) prior to a disposal to ensure the property was a main residence.

However, recent decisions have made it clear that the courts are taking a pretty inconsistent view on this and the way this subject has developed it is going to be very difficult indeed for a property to qualify as a residence at all.

We might start with Lord Widgery's celebrated description of a residence:

"A place where a man is based or where he continues to live, the place where he sleeps and shelters and has his home. It is imperative to remember in this context that residence implies a degree of permanence. Consequently, a person is not entitled to claim to be resident merely because he pays a short temporary visit. Some assumption of permanence, some degree of continuity,

some expectation of continuity is a vital factor which turns simple occupation into residence."

This approach was adopted by the Court of Appeal in Goodwin v Curtis, although in that case the taxpayer only occupied the property for five weeks. He had just separated from his wife and stayed in the property as temporary accommodation - and two days after moving in he purchased another property which he intended to be his main residence. He lost.

That seems fair enough until we get to the recent case of Susan Bradley v HMRC who separated from her husband, moved out of the matrimonial home and moved into another house that she owned.

She made some improvements and generally made it more of a home. Although she put the property on the market, the market was very poor and she expected to live there permanently. After eight months she was reconciled with her husband and moved back into the matrimonial home. The tribunal found that her occupation was only temporary; she had put it on the market and it was never her residence at all.

CHAPTER 3

HOW PPR RELIEF AND LETTINGS RELIEF WORKS

Where an individual has occupied a property as a residence for only part of his period of ownership then a proportion of the capital gain resulting on the disposal of the property is exempt. This is calculated on the following basis:

Capital gain x period of occupation/period of ownership

In addition to the period that an individual actually occupies a property as his residence, when calculating the period of occupation there are certain deemed periods of occupation which are allowed to be taken into account.

In all cases before 6 April 2014 the last 36 months of ownership would be deemed to be occupied by you irrespective of whether you actually occupied the property during this period.

As well as PPR relief, if the property has been let you may be entitled to lettings relief.

Where a property is let then clearly the owner won't be able to establish the property as his main residence for this period.

However, a form of relief ('lettings relief') is available.

An exemption from capital gains tax is granted for that part of the gain attributable to the letting in so far as it does not exceed the lower of :

- the tax free part of the gain under the PPR relief
- £40,000

Therefore if you had a property that was to be let, you could occupy it as a residence either before or after the letting and make the necessary PPR relief claim.

You would then be entitled to partial PPR relief and lettings relief.

Example

Johnny has owned his property for 10 years. He has lived in it since the purchase date. He is buying another property and will sell his old main residence in 5 years time.

If the gain on disposal was £100,000 his gain after PPR relief and Letting relief will be:

PPR relief =
Period of ownership = 15 years

Period of occupation = 10 years + last 3 years deemed occupation (assuming the pre April 2014 rules applied)

PPR relief = 13/15 * £100,000 = £86,667

Lettings relief is the lower of:

PPR relief = £66,667
£40,000

As the gain after PPR relief is only £13,333, Lettings Relief would eliminate the remaining gain to Zero. No capital loss could be created.

Other deemed periods

As well as the final 36 months/18 months deemed occupation, there are other periods of absence that can be treated as being occupied.

The additional deemed periods are only possible where the individual is absent from the property and he has no other residence eligible for PPR.

There is no minimum period of occupation for PPR relief but usually the house has to be physically occupied as a residence before and after any period of absence unless the reason for the absence was that the owner was working away, then he does not have to return to the house if his work subsequently requires residence elsewhere.

Three specific periods of absence qualify as 'deemed occupation':

1. Any period of absence – maximum three years.
2. Overseas employment of himself or spouse/civil partner – unlimited period.
3. Employment elsewhere (employed or self-employed) of himself or spouse/civil partner – maximum four years.

Changes from 5 April 2014

As from 6 April 2014 the final 36 months of deemed occupation is reduced to 18 months.

Note that it doesn't matter when you started to occupy the property when looking at this change in the rules. It is the date of disposal that is important.

If the disposal is after 5 April 2014 there will only be a final deemed occupation period of 18 months.

This will reduce the amount of PPR relief for anyone who has left more than 18 months between ceasing to occupy a property and selling it.

There will also be an additional consequence that could see the amount of Lettings Relief also reduced.

Lettings Relief is based on the lower of:

- The amount of PPR relief
- The gain attributable to the letting
- £40,000

Therefore assuming the amounts are less than £40,000 the reduction in PPR relief could also lead to less Lettings Relief –

dependent on the gain attributable to the letting.

CHAPTER 4

PPR RELIEF WHERE YOU HAVE TWO OR MORE HOMES

When a person owns two properties a popular method to obtain PPR relief twice is to use the PPR election to nominate one of the properties as a main residence.

To make the election you need to have two or more residences -- not just two or more properties. The difference between a property and a residence is an important difference. A residence is essentially somewhere that:

- You own an interest in, and
- You actually occupy

Therefore firstly you need to either own the freehold or own a leasehold interest. If you occupy a property as a licence it won't qualify.

So if for example you live with your friend in his house and pay no contribution to the bills etc you couldn't class this as a residence and make a PPR election in favour of another property that you did actually own.

Secondly you need to actually occupy a property. Just having the intention to occupy won't be sufficient (with an exception being if you actually live in job related accommodation and then purchase your own property which you intend to occupy).

So if you rent out a property you own you've got no chance of classing this as a residence for that period if you clearly aren't occupying it. So when can you make the election?

Well to make the election usually you would be in the position of actually owning two properties, with one occupied weekdays and the other at weekends.

The Revenue traditionally accept that a city 'crash pad' occupied Monday to Friday and a separate family home occupied Friday evening to Sunday would be classed as two residences. Therefore the PPR election could be made.

Another example could simply be a property occupied every month or so for a short break. Note though there must be some degree of permanency and occupation for only a handful of days each year wouldn't qualify.

In the case of an MP for instance they would have a constituency property and also a London property. Both would be occupied during the year by the MP but at different times. They may for instance live in one for 4 days a week and then return to their family for the remainder of the week. They can make a PPR election to choose which property is their main residence for the purpose of claiming PPR relief.

This could apply to you if you occupy one property as your main home and also occupy the other on a regular basis (eg Monthly for a few days).

What is the benefit of making the PPR election?

Being able to make a PPR election can be a very valuable as the property that you choose doesn't have to actually be the main residence. This gives great flexibility as it essentially allows you to pick and choose which property will get some PPR relief, so you can ensure that properties with the highest gain qualify for relief and minimise your CGT charge.

This is even more beneficial when you understand just how PPR relief operates.

When a property has been a main residence, it automatically qualifies for PPR relief for the last 36 months (reducing to 18 months from April 2014). As PPR relief operates on a time apportioned basis this means that even if you make a property your main residence for one day you'll get the last 36/18 months exempt.

How to benefit from the use of the PPR election

Where you own two properties which are occupied by you as residences you'll be able to submit a PPR election to determine which property is the main residence for capital gains tax purposes.

Here's a good example to illustrate the points.

Example

Steve owns a house in Yarmouth West which he occupies for 4 days a week and a London flat which he uses when he's working in London

He is looking at selling one of the properties. The capital gain to date on the Yarmouth house is £50,000, and the gain on the London flat is £150,000.

He's owed the Yarmouth property for 1 year and the London flat for three years.

He decides to make a PPR relief election in favour of the London flat. This therefore nominates this property as the main residence and this will then qualify for PPR relief.

He disposes of the Yarmouth house first. Steve can therefore vary his election, and elect the Yarmouth property as his main residence for a nominal period eg 1 month, before reelecting the London flat.

The benefit of this is that the Yarmouth property will be the main residence for that 1 month period, and this property will then qualify for the last 36 months of PPR relief exemption (based on the pre April 2014 rules). As such the £50,000 gain on the Yarmouth property will be fully exempt from CGT with only a potential loss of relief on the London flat of 1 month.

If he'd not made the PPR election and had just had the London flat as his main residence this would have cost him an extra £14,000 in CGT (assuming the annual exemption was already used up).

Note that as from April 2014 the reduction in the final period of occupation to 18 months, therefore Steve would need to sell the Yarmouth property within 18 months of his purchase date to qualify for full PPR relief following the nomination.

However, the benefit is that making the PPR election allows you to choose which of your properties is to be the main residence and you can then vary this to ensure that each property gets some PPR relief whilst making use of the deemed 18/36 months occupation for each property.

Note that if you are married you would both need to make the PPR election as a married couple would need to both have the same main residence.

Can I use the PPR election?

Absolutely! Providing you take care as to the requirements in terms of ensuring:

- You own an interest in the property, and
- You actually occupy the property as a residence

You'll be able to make use of this technique to reduce capital gains tax

Once you've actually met these requirements you then need to make the election.

The key issue here is the time limit. You've got a strict time limit of two years from the date you have a combination of residences, and the Revenue do stick to this pretty rigorously.

There is no particular format for the election, although a letter stating the addresses of the two residences, dates of purchase, your tax references and the property to be treated as the PPR would be sufficient. You should also state the date that the property would be treated as the PPR from.

Here is a sample PPR election you may like to use:

Sample PPR election

To

Your Address

H M Inspector of Taxes
{Insert Tax office address}

Insert Date

Dear Sir

TAX REFERENCE – XXX/XXXXXXXXX

PRINCIPAL PRIVATE RESIDENCE RELIEF ELECTION

Please accept this letter of notice of my intention to elect under S222(5) TCGA 1992 the property as detailed below as my main residence for the period stated. I further confirm that this election is made within the two year time limit as specified in S222(5)(a) TCGA 1992.

Property details

Property Number/Name and Address:

Date of Purchase:

Date occupied as a residence from :

Period this property is be treated as the main residence for:

Your Faithfully

{Name}

CHAPTER 5

OFFSETTING LOSSES ON A MAIN RESIDENCE AND MAXIMISING TAX RELIEF

With the substantial drop in property prices, and with some areas not forecast to return to 2007 price levels until 2018 many people may be selling properties at a loss.

Making full use of that loss, will be crucial, particularly given the current low property levels also present many opportunities for investors to realise large capital gains. In this chapter we look at capital losses on property disposals and in particular how this is affected if you've previously occupied the property.

Capital losses

The general rule is that when you sell a property at a loss you will be treated as crystallising a capital loss based on the proceeds less the cost of the property.

Remember that you can deduct the incidental expenses of buying and selling the property. So you'll also be able to deduct stamp duty on purchase, and the legal and estate agents fees in buying and selling the property.

If you've incurred capital expenditure on enhancing or improving the property you can also deduct these to increase your capital loss. So if you've put in a new kitchen, bathroom etc make sure you claim for the costs you incurred.

One point to watch out for though is that enhancement costs need to be reflected in the property at the date of disposal. So if you put a bathroom in 5 years ago and then replaced it with another one 2 years ago you won't be able to claim for the old one you put in 5 years ago.

The annual CGT exemption isn't offset to increase the capital gain.

Your capital loss is then offset against any other capital gains in the current year, and if not fully utilised would then be carried forward indefinitely for offset against other capital gains.

A couple of points to bear in mind on the loss offset:

- Firstly when carried forward it is only offset to bring your gains down to the annual exemption. This therefore ensures that your capital losses aren't wasted. This doesn't apply for current year gains though so if you have a choice realising a capital gain in the year after the loss is realised, rather than in the year of the loss could be beneficial
- Secondly clogged losses can only be offset against clogged gains. Clogged losses are losses on disposals to connected people (eg parents, siblings, children etc). The basic rule is that such a loss can only be set off against gains which:

  - arise from other disposals (in the same or a later year) to that same person; and
  - arise at a time when the persons concerned are still connected.

Note that capital losses cannot be offset against income.

Capital losses on a property you have occupied

If you've occupied a property as a main residence at any point you'll be entitled to claim principal private residence ('PPR') relief to reduce the capital gain. The corollary to this is that any loss on the disposal of the property could be restricted.

In any case where a property would qualify for principal private residence relief the computation of the loss and the restriction of that loss are dealt with in the same way as the computation of a gain and the restriction of that gain.

Therefore your loss would be restricted based on the proportion of the ownership that you have occupied the property for.

So, essentially losses and gains are treated the same for PPR relief purposes and PPR relief will reduce not only gains but also losses.

As PPR relief is based on:

Period of occupation/Period of ownership

You'll find that capital losses are reduced by this fraction as well.

You should also bear in mind that the last 18/36 months are deemed to be occupied by you where the property has been your main residence at any point, so this will further reduce the loss offset.

Example

As an example if you bought a house in June 2005 for £200,000 occupied it for 1 year and then sold it for £100,000 in June 2014 you'd have a loss before PPR relief of £100,000.

PPR relief would be:

Period of ownership = 9 years
Period of occupation = 1 year + last 18 months deemed occupation
= 2.5 years PPR relief = 2.5/9 * 100,000 = £27,778.

Therefore the available capital loss would be £72,222.

Lettings relief

If you have a property that has been occupied as a main residence and was also let you can usually claim lettings relief to further reduce the capital gain.

Does this also apply in the case of a loss to further reduce the loss?

The Revenue state not. Lettings relief which is available when all or part of a person's residence is let, restricts the capital gain based on three limits.

If no gain arises the limits cannot be applied. So the limits cannot be used to restrict a loss.

Therefore if you make a loss on the disposal of a property you've occupied as a main residence that loss would not be an allowable loss to the extent that private residence relief is available. There is though no further restriction of the allowable loss for lettings relief.

CHAPTER 6

POINTS TO WATCH OUT FOR WHEN SELLING A FORMER MAIN RESIDENCE AFTER YOU'VE LEFT THE UK

It's a pretty common scenario. You own your own home in the UK, which you occupy as your main residence. At a later date you decide to emigrate, either permanently or for a temporary period.

During this period overseas you may well let the property out, but there is likely to come a time when you decide to sell it.

The key question is whether the UK taxman will want a slice of any profits, and if so how much will they want.

The fact that any proceeds were reinvested into either a new residence or even a business operation is irrelevant from a UK perspective. A capital gain would arise on any the disposal of the property based on the uplift in value since acquisition and after taking account of any expenses incurred on the property.

There are broadly speaking two key options for reducing or eliminating the gain.

Non residence

Firstly there is the non resident status to consider.

An individual who is non UK resident is outside the scope of UK CGT on his worldwide disposals. This means that no gain would be charged on a disposal of the UK property.

Note that the 2013 Autumn Statement included provisions to change this from April 2015 so that CGT is applied to disposals of UK investment property by non UK residents. However, they are consulting on this change during 2014.

Based on the current rules you would need to ensure that your period of non UK residence during which you sold the property was for at least five or six tax years (depending on your date of departure) in order to prevent the gain being charged on your return to the UK.

Therefore if you are non UK resident and satisfy these provisions the use of the property is irrelevant and you would be automatically exempt from UK tax.

One point you would need to watch out for is whether you are established as a resident of another country. If you are, you would need to consider their tax rules, and in particular whether they would tax the gain.

If you have been overseas for more than five years but are looking at returning to the UK, it would make sense to look at whether you should bring forward a disposal date to crystallise the gain before you become UK resident.

Even if you did not want to actually dispose of the property before you returned to the UK (for example you may want to stay there on your return) you could consider a transfer of the property to a close family member/ friend or to a controlled company.

The benefit in this is that it would uplift the base cost to the market value at the date of the transfer. On a future disposal of the property any gain that would arise (and be subject to UK tax) would be vastly reduced. In fact if a disposal was shortly after your return the gain could in any case be covered by the annual CGT exemption.

If you were to remain overseas for less than five/six years or if you were retain the property and dispose of it after becoming UK resident, some valuable reliefs would be given if this was your principal private residence. The CGT annual exemption would also be available to offset any gain, but this is minimal (currently £11,000 pa).

The main relief available in this case will be principal private residence ('PPR') relief.

PPR relief

The extent of PPR relief, will depend on the occupation of the property.

Where an individual has occupied a property as a residence for only part of his period of ownership then a proportion of the capital gain resulting on the disposal of the property is exempt. This is calculated on the following basis:

Capital gain x period of occupation/period of ownership

In addition to the period that an individual actually occupies a property as his residence, when calculating the period of occupation there are certain deemed periods of occupation which are allowed to be taken into account.

As from 6 April 2014 the last 18 months of ownership would be deemed to be occupied by you irrespective of whether you actually occupied the property during this period.

This applies to everyone. So if you occupied a property as a main residence, then went away for one year and sold it after one year of absence the gain would be exempt under the PPR relief provisions whether you were UK resident or not.

If your absence was for more than 18 months you may also be able to claim the entire period you worked overseas as deemed occupation of the property. This is an additional exemption and will apply where you lived in the property both before and after your period overseas, where you went overseas to work under a full time employment, and where you had no other residence overseas.

This is only likely to be the case where you occupy property overseas either as employer provided accommodation or under a form of licence (ie no tenancy). If you did have a residence overseas this further exemption wouldn't be available although the Revenue may accept an election from your to nominate the UK property as your main residence.

In either of these two cases this would mean that your UK house would still qualify for full PPR relief when you sold it. However even if it didn't more reliefs could be offset.

As well as principal private residence ('PPR') relief where a property is let you would also be able to claim lettings relief to reduce the gain.

Therefore whether you dispose of a property as a non UK resident or as a UK resident you should be able to claim significant relief.

If your period abroad lasts at least five/six tax years, and the overseas regime does not tax the gain, it would make sense to aim for a transfer to a connected party to achieve an uplift in the base cost.

Even if you don't meet the five/six year requirement as a former main residence you can qualify for some significant reliefs.

As stated earlier in the chapter though, there are proposals to change the CGT position for non-residents from April 2015. We will need to wait and see what impact these rule changes will have.

CHAPTER 7

HOW TO AVOID TAXES IF YOU'RE SELLING PART OF YOUR GARDEN

Given the relatively 'easy' money that can be made by selling land to a property developer, the tax implications of a disposal of part of your garden becomes of increasing importance.

The disposal of land is a chargeable disposal for capital gains tax ('CGT') purposes. However the key consideration in tax terms will be whether principal private residence ('PPR') relief will operate.

Where an individual has occupied a property as a residence either wholly or partly for their period of ownership then a proportion of the capital gain resulting on the disposal of the property is exempt.

This is calculated on the following basis:

Capital gain x period of occupation/period of ownership

However, when a residence has gardens or grounds with it, the extent of the garden or grounds of a person's residence which automatically qualifies for relief is 0.5 hectares (approx 1.25 acres).

In other words if the garden or grounds do not exceed this area relief for the whole of the garden or grounds is automatically due.

Therefore the first consideration when considering a disposal of your garden should be the size of the garden/grounds in question. If they are less than 1.25 acres there should be no problem with the disposal as HMRC traditionally accept that this would be covered by PPR relief.

If the garden or grounds exceed this relief may be available for a larger area if the grounds are required for the reasonable enjoyment of the dwelling house as a residence, having regard to the size and character of the dwelling house.

This is frequently a matter that will be looked at by the district valuer, and he will bear in mind:

- the size and character of the dwelling house
- what part of that dwelling house has been used as its owner's residence.
- what land is required for the reasonable enjoyment of that residence.

Note that the permitted area (ie the area that meets the reasonable use and enjoyment test) is a specific area, and as well as determining the extent of the permitted area the District Valuer will determine where the permitted area is.

Each disposal of a piece of land which has been part of the garden or grounds of a residence can attract private residence relief if some or all of the land sold falls within the permitted area.

Therefore a key issue will be to determine the extent and location of the 'permitted area' for your property, to assess whether the land disposal will fall within this area. If it does PPR relief will, in principle, be available.

Aside from simply selling the land to a developer, a further option would be to actually undertake the development yourself and subcontract the work to local builders.

The potential profits are greater but what we're really concerned with are the post tax profits. For example its better to make £100K tax free, than £150K that is taxed at 40%.

As regards the building of a new property the first point to consider would be how this activity will be treated for tax purposes. There are broadly two options, either treat it as a capital transaction or as a trading transaction.

If the intention in developing the the property was to develop and sell the property with the intention of making a profit, HMRC could argue that you were a property trader.

By contrast capital transactions are usually retained for property investments, eg an individual purchasing a property to rent out.

The distinction impacts on how any 'profit' is treated and taxed. A property trader would be subject to income tax on any profit, whereas the disposal of a property investment would be subject to capital gains tax ('CGT') on any gain arising.

In some circumstances trader treatment can be beneficial, particularly as it allows for a greater offset of expenses and losses. Whether HMRC would agree to capital or trading treatment will depend on a number of issues, including:

- Whether you have undertaken this kind of activity before
- How long the property will be held prior to disposal
- Will the property be rented out
- Whether you anticipate doing this again

However it would be rare that trader treatment would be preferred.

As such if possible you'd be looking to argue for capital treatment.

If they accept that this is a capital transaction, this would allow the offset of the various CGT reliefs such as the annual exemption and PPR relief etc.

Occupation of the new property as a residence would be beneficial as this could allow principal private residence ('PPR') relief to be offset. In addition if you decided to let the property also lettings relief.

Lettings relief can be very advantageous as it provides for a further capital gains tax deduction of up to £40,000. This is however restricted to the amount of PPR relief and the gain that is attributable to the letting.

One option if a full development of a new property is envisaged would be to build a new property and then move into this permanently. Provided the 'old' main residence is sold within 18 months of the date that they move into the new property there would be no CGT charge.

Similarly provided the new property is occupied for a sufficient period to make it a main residence there should be no CGT charge on a future disposal of this.

Recent HMRC attack on PPR relief

HMRC are now pursuing another tack which appeared in the recent Dickinson case.

"A" had a house and garden which included a tennis court. She sold part of the tennis court to a developer. HMRC claimed that this disposal did not benefit from PPR relief which provides an exemption for the disposal of:

a) a dwelling house or part of a dwelling house which is, or has at any time in his period of ownership being, his only or main residence, or

b) land which he has for his own occupation and enjoyment with that residence as its garden or grounds up to the permitted area.

HMRC argued that when the land was sold "A" no longer had the land for her own occupation or enjoyment with her residence because it had become a building site and could no longer be regarded as garden or grounds.

It is relevant to this argument that (a) above refers to the dwelling house which is, or has at any time during his period of ownership been, his only or main residence, whereas (b) refers to "land which he has for his own occupation and enjoyment". The use of the present tense means that the occupation and enjoyment of the land must continue until the moment of sale.

The thinking here is well understood.

If you have a house and you sell part of your garden then the gain on that disposal qualifies for the exemption. If however, you sell a house and most of the garden but hang to a bit of garden and sell it later, the subsequent sale of that piece of land will not qualify for the relief because it is not a residence and neither is it the garden or grounds of a residence - the residence has already gone.

However, in the case of Dickinson "A" was still living in the house and certainly the tennis court had been part of her garden or grounds - it was just that before contracts were exchanged, she let the developers in to dig up the tennis court. HMRC said this meant it was no longer part of her garden or grounds and relief should be denied.

The Tribunal rejected the HMRC view. As such "A"was entitled to PPR relief.

CHAPTER 8

CLAIMING PRINCIPAL PRIVATE RESIDENCE RELIEF IF YOU CONVERT A HOUSE INTO FLATS

The key relief when you are looking at converting a residential house into flats may be principal private residence relief.

The tax legislation states that Principal Private Residence relief is available where a gain arises from the disposal of an interest in a dwelling house or part of a dwelling house which has at some time been its owners only or main residence.

In most cases the whole of a building in which an individual lives will be a dwelling house. But in some cases the dwelling house may be more than one building or only part of a building.

If you have converted a house into flats it would therefore need to be considered what constituted the 'dwelling house' - either the entire property or just the individuals flats.

The commonest example of a dwelling house which is only part of a building in which it is situated is a flat in a block of flats. Each flat is a self-contained unit and is itself regarded as a dwelling house and not part of a dwelling house.

The Revenue have stated:

'...There are also buildings which to outward appearances are a single dwelling house but which are in fact split up into self-contained units. Each self-contained unit is itself a dwelling house...'

If therefore each flat had separate facilities such as bathroom, kitchen, bedrooms, etc there would be little prospect of arguing that they were not separate dwelling houses.

On this basis in order to obtain PPR relief on the disposal of the flats you would have needed to have actually occupied them as a main residence. If for example you were to occupy a flat for a period as a main residence before moving into one of the other flats you could then claim PPR relief on the disposal.

Therefore if you converted a house into 3 flats and you occupied flat 1 and then flat 2 these would qualify for PPR relief on a disposal. This is based on the ratio of:

Period of occupation/Period of ownership

In both cases the last 18 months of ownership would be deemed to be occupied by you.

In addition in respect of the two flats that you actually occupied as a main residence you could claim lettings relief if they were let at any point in your period of ownership.

This would provide for a further exemption for the lower of:

- £40,000
- PPR relief
- The gain attributable to the letting

In essence therefore if each flat is regarded as a separate dwelling house you would need to apportion the gain between the flats sold and then calculate PPR relief and lettings relief for the disposal of flats actually occupied (eg 1 & 2).

The gains would then all be consolidated and the annual exemption would then be offset to provide your chargeable gain.

Any flats that you didn't occupy could be faced with a CGT charge on the disposal. It's also worth noting that there is anti avoidance legislation that can prevent PPR relief applying where there is expenditure incurred for the purposes of realizing a gain. As such renting or occupying the property would assist in demonstrating that this was not the case.

If you can obtain full PPR relief on the disposal it would not need to be disclosed to the Revenue.

CHAPTER 9

TAX IMPLICATIONS OF LETTING FAMILY LIVE IN YOUR PROPERTY

Lots of people let family or close friends live in their property for a period. In this chapter we look at the tax implications as well as tax planning opportunities that could arise in this scenario.

Capital Gains Tax

One of the key implications will be capital gains tax. Under normal circumstances if you've owned and lived in a property you'll obtain principal private residence relief on the disposal. However if you've let a friend or relative live there and you have ceased to occupy it you'll start to lose PPR relief.

PPR relief operates based on the period that you occupied a property, in comparison to the period that you owned it for.

Therefore if you moved out and let someone else live in it you would start to lose relief. The main exception to this is when you move out and then sell it within 18 months. In this case you'd be fully exempt from CGT even if you never set foot in it for 18 months and let a relative live there.

If you were to let a relative live in a property in capital gains tax terms it would be much more beneficial to charge them a rental for living there, rather than to simply let them live there for free.

The rent would not need to be a market rent, but if a rent was charged and the property was leased to them (and that a tenancy agreement etc was in place) you'd be able to claim lettings relief when the property is sold.

Note this assumes that you used to live in the property, and have since moved out and allowed someone else to live there. It's essential to claiming lettings relief that you have occupied the property as a main residence at some point.

Assuming this is the case, you'll be able to claim lettings relief to reduce the gain by an amount up to the lower of:

- the amount of PPR relief
- £40,000
- the gain attributable to the letting of the property

Therefore providing you moved out and immediately let a friend or relative lease the property any gain remaining after PPR relief should represent the gain attributable to the letting.

If you have let a friend or relative live in the property at the same time as you (eg they use one bedroom and share other facilities) there should be no restriction in the capital gain.

Even if they were paying for their stay the Revenue allow one 'lodger' to live with you in the property sharing the household facilities without there being a restriction in PPR relief.

Income tax

You do not have to charge a rental for the use of the property, and if you do decide to charge a rental there is no requirement for this to be a market rent. You could therefore charge a nominal rental for their use of the property.

Any rent that you do receive though would be subject to income tax.

The main exception to this is if you are living in the property and let a family member use the property along with you. In this case you can claim an income tax exemption for any receipts up to £4,250 under the rent a room scheme.

Inheritance tax

If the property is owned by you it would be included in your estate, irrespective of who lives there. However if a relative lives with you in the property there is a potential benefit in that you could transfer an interest in the property without being subject to the gift with reservation of benefit provisions.

This is important because usually where you actually occupy a property any attempt to transfer it to someone else would be fruitless in terms of inheritance tax, as the full value would still remain in your estate.

However, if you have someone who lives with you and pays their share of the bills (in a form of co-occupation scenario) you can transfer a share to them without being caught by these provisions which will therefore reduce the value of your estate. Given that for many people their house is their largest asset this can represent a significant tax saving.

CHAPTER 10

AVOIDING TAX ON THE TRANSFER OF PROPERTY TO CHILDREN

Many people want to pass assets and in particular property onto their children. This could be in the hope of avoiding inheritance tax or simply as a means to give children a 'good start' in life. Any transfer of property will however have tax implications and these should be carefully considered.

Capital gains tax

Lets look first at the capital gains tax position of a transfer of property.

On the assumption that the parent is UK resident and domiciled any transfer of property will be subject to UK capital gains tax.

You'll therefore need to calculate the gain arising and crucially to consider the offset of reliefs to reduce this gain.

It's worth noting that the residence of the child is irrelevant for UK tax purposes.

Therefore, even if they are tax resident in a tax haven, the UK resident and domiciled parent will still have to consider their own capital gains tax position.

As parents are classed as 'connected' with their children for capital gains tax purposes, any transfer from the parents to the child is treated as a market value transfer.

As such, even though the children don't pay any proceeds to the parent for the property, when calculating the capital gain it is the market value of the property that needs to be considered.

The gain will therefore represent the uplift in value from the date of acquisition or probate value to the market value at the date of transfer. Note if the property was acquired before March 1982 there are special provisions that can apply to deem the cost to be the market value at March 1982.

What reliefs are offset?

There are some reliefs that can apply, but these tend to be in very limited circumstances.

The main reliefs that any parent would be looking to consider to reduce the capital gain would be:

Gift relief. If a property is used for the purposes of the parents trade or their trading company they may be able to claim gift relief. This allows a deferral of the gain arising (provided the child agrees!) and allows the parent to pass the property to the child free of capital gains tax. The future disposal of the property by the child would then crystallise the deferred capital gain.

Annual exemption. If the parents own the property jointly the humble annual capital gains tax exemption should not be forgotten. It allows each individual to exempt (currently) £11,000 of any gains from capital gains tax in each tax year. So if the parents had no other capital gains, the annual exemption could ensure that a gain of £22,000 was fully exempt from tax.

Other capital gains tax exemptions such as rollover relief and the EIS deferral relief would not apply as there are no disposal proceeds!

Non UK resident parents

If the parents are non UK resident they can transfer foreign property to their children free of CGT subject to two key points:

1. If you own the property at the date you leave the UK you'll need to ensure that you remain non UK resident for more than five complete tax years to avoid UK capital gains tax. If you come back before this the capital gain will be charged in the tax year of your return.

2. As mentioned earlier in the book, there are proposals to bring non UK residents within the scope of UK CGT on UK property disposals from April 2015.

Inheritance tax

Any transfer at undervalue from the parents to the children will usually be a potentially exempt transfer ('PET') for inheritance tax purposes.

So in the case of a gift of the property the full market value of the property will be treated as a PET. If the children were to pay some of the value to the parents it would only be the difference between the market value and the amount paid that would be a PET.

With a PET there is no immediate Inheritance tax charge on the parents and provided they survive for at least seven years from the date of the transfer the amount gifted would be excluded from their estates for inheritance tax purposes.

Note that the residence and domicile status of the children is again irrelevant.

Non Resident parents

Non UK resident parents would have no impact on the Inheritance tax position, and the transfer would still be a PET for inheritance tax purposes.

Gift with reservation of benefit rules

If the parents make a gift to the children and retain a benefit in the property transferred there are special anti avoidance rules than can ensure that the property is not classed as a PET for Inheritance tax purposes.

Instead the property remains within their estate for Inheritance tax purposes until the benefit ceases. This could apply for instance if the parents continue to live in the property, of if they continue to benefit from the rental income obtained from the property.

One way that they could get around having the property still in their estate would be to pay the children a market rate for the benefit that they get from the property (eg market rental).

Stamp duty Land Tax

Unless the property is mortgaged the parents should be able to transfer the property to the children free of stamp duty providing it is a genuine gift.

If there was any proceeds payable to the parents this would then be classed as 'chargeable consideration' for stamp duty purposes and a stamp duty charge would need to be calculated.

Note that if there is a mortgage or any other form of debt that is transferred from parents to the children with the property this would also be classed as 'consideration' for the purposes of stamp duty.

CHAPTER 11

HOW TO CLAIM PPR RELIEF ON PROPERTY OCCUPIED BY A RELATIVE

When looking at the capital gains tax position on the disposal of property, the beneficial interest can have a significant impact.

CGT follows primarily the beneficial, as opposed to the legal interest. So the title holder is not necessarily the one subject to CGT on the disposal. Good examples of this are bare trustees and nominees.

So if you have a case where A, is the legal owner but holds the property as a nominee or bare trustee for B, on a disposal of the property it is B that is subject to CGT. Similarly there is no CGT charge on any transfer of the legal interest from A to B.

This, or at least variations on this, are very common. There are many instances where a property is held legally by one individual but actually occupied by another. In this case unless you can show that the occupier of the property actually held the beneficial interest, any capital gain on disposal would arise to the legal owner and would be subject to CGT.

By contrast if the occupier was subject to CGT they may well qualify for a CGT exemption under the principal private residence ('PPR') relief rules.

So determining the beneficial interest can be very important for CGT purposes.

In many cases the beneficial interest will depend on who has the 'rights and responsibilities of ownership'. This will include the responsibility for bills, ability to occupy it, ability to determine when it is sold, benefiting from the proceeds of sale etc.

If you wanted to argue that property was held as a nominee or bare trustee it is usually advisable to back all this up with a nominee agreement specifically stating who holds the beneficial interest in the property.

Occupation by an elderly relative

This argument was used in a recent case where they successfully claimed principal private residence relief from capital gains tax on the sale of a flat occupied by an elderly parent.

The flat was originally owned by the individuals' (A's) mother/mother-in-law. She had sold it to A subject to an agreement permitting her to remain in occupation for life or until remarriage (a small amount of consideration was paid by the mother/mother-in-law to remain in occupation and she was to pay for insurance, repairs and all outgoings). The flat was later sold when she could no longer manage the stairs and more suitable accommodation was found for her.

It was found that, in acquiring the flat on terms which included the agreement, A (and A's spouse) were were assuming the role of trustees. They did not become absolutely entitled to the flat with the exclusive right to direct how the flat should be dealt with. A's subsequent actions in dealing with the property clearly showed that they had accepted obligations associated with a trust and the role of trustee. Their interest was a 'settled interest' for which principal private residence relief was available.

This could be a useful argument in other cases where property is to be occupied by an elderly relative. Other considerations would also need to be taken into account (eg the beneficial interest would then form part of their estate for IHT purposes).

CHAPTER 12

BUYING PROPERTY TAX EFFICIENTLY WHILST YOUR CHILDREN ARE STUDYING

The slump in property prices will have made many people consider whether buying property for their children to occupy whilst at university is cost effective.

However, given the currently low prices, if you're looking at the long term with perhaps other family members occupying the property and also renting it out to third parties it can still be a worthwhile investment.

If you were looking to structure such an investment you have three main options:

- Firstly you could purchase in your name
- Secondly you could purchase in your child's name
- Thirdly you could use a trust

Purchasing in your name

If you purchase in your name you obviously have total control over the property, however it is generally a tax inefficient option.

As you haven't occupied the property as a main residence you won't get principal private residence ('PPR') relief on a disposal. In addition the property will remain within your estate for inheritance tax purposes.

Purchasing in your children's name

There is an immediate inheritance tax advantage as after 7 years the value gifted will be excluded from your estate (provided you don't continue to benefit from the property).

However the PPR relief position would not be straightforward. If you purchased in the name of one of your children they would only obtain PPR relief to reduce the gain on a disposal for the period that they actually occupied the property. If they occupied the property for say 4 years and then another sibling occupied it there would not be total relief from tax on the disposal.

Even if you purchased the property in multiple names unless they all occupied the property for the entire period of ownership (except for the final 18 months) there would not be full PPR relief. The other disadvantage of purchasing in your children's name is that they would have full control over the property (although you could mitigate this with a charge over the property).

Using a trust

In most cases using a trust would be a very attractive option. It provides for flexibility in terms of the occupation, gives you some element of control and also has significant tax advantages.

Consider the following arrangement:

- You establish a trust and transfer funds into it to buy a property;
- Trustees are appointed to manage the trust - these can be family members if you choose, but you can also appoint a Trustee Company, which is set up specifically to act as a professional trustee
- The trust purchases a property for £300,000 which is then occupied by "child-one" as his / her principal private residence for three years;
- On graduating "child-one" moves out and the property is let for two years until "child-two" moves in;
- "Child-two" then occupies for four further years;

The property is then let for six years and finally sold for a gain of £200,000 after ownership for 15 years.

The main benefit is terms of Capital Gains Tax. Assuming CGT is paid at 28%, the tax due would vary considerably. If the property had been bought by:

a. you, the tax would be £44,800;
b. your child, it would be £22,400;
c. the trust, it would be £NIL.

As the property is occupied by more than one beneficiary this enables the trust to benefit from a number of aspects of the principal private residence relief whilst also benefiting from letting relief.

The occupation by two children as beneficiaries of the trust enables the trust to relieve a much greater percentage of the chargeable gain and, in this instance, all that remains is then mitigated by letting relief.

If the trust excludes you, then the amount settled by you will drop out of your estate for Inheritance Tax (IHT) purposes after seven years.

However, if IHT planning is not an objective of this arrangement, then all the family, including yourself, can be beneficiaries of the trust without losing the CGT advantages and everyone can benefit under the terms of the trust when it comes to dividing up the proceeds.

Another issue is what happens to the property if not sold. Your first child may have married, and even entered into a divorce. If the capital is advanced when the proceeds are realised, then on divorce, half of the capital would be lost.

If instead, the trustees loan the capital to "child one", then on the dissolution of the marriage the capital can be recovered (as it is a debt to the trust) and, at a later date, the capital can be advanced directly to "child one"

CHAPTER 13

HELPING YOUR CHILDREN TO BUY THEIR FIRST PROPERTY TAX EFFICIENTLY

For a variety of reasons many adult children aren't able to get on the property ladder without some financial help from their parents.

If you're considering ways to help your children buy their first home it's important that you consider the tax implications both for you and your children.

In particular parents in the baby boomer generation are also looking at the value of their own assets and becoming increasingly worried about Inheritance Tax (IHT) on their estates when they pass away. The credit crunch affects them too as the new Government coalition has put on hold all prospect of increasing the IHT threshold at any time in the near future.

Options

Making a loan

One of the easiest options is to give a loan to your children. This should be evidenced in a written loan agreement and should be secured on the property.

The loan would remain within the parents estate for IHT purposes, and if they were to waive the loan at any point this would be a potentially exempt transfer which would then be excluded from their estate after 7 tax years.

The loan could be interest free or set at a low rate of interest. Any interest repayments would be taxable on the parents but the capital element would be free of tax.

The parents would no interest in the actual property which would allow the child to occupy it and claim a subsequent exemption from capital gains tax on the disposal.

Note that any mortgage company lending the rest of the purchase price will require their money back first so if prices fall and disaster strikes, parents may not get their money back.

Pay grandchildren's school or childcare costs

Parents can make gifts of surplus income without incurring a charge to IHT.

The gifts need to be made regularly -- not one-off -- and the parents need to show that they have surplus income over their expenditure needs. This can be flexible -- if the parents' income needs change, the gifts can be reduced or stopped.

To get the IHT exemption, detailed records of income and expenses need to be kept.

Everybody has an annual allowance for IHT of £3,000 so both parents can make yearly gifts up to this sum without a charge to tax. They can also make one-off small gifts of up to £250 to individuals

By making tax efficient gifts of income to cover others costs of the children, they can then meet their own mortgage costs.

Make a pre-inheritance gift to the children

Parents need to be sure they can afford to release the capital now and in the future. Pension provisions must be sufficient to fund retirement needs notwithstanding the possibility of investment swings.

A gift now starts the clock ticking - live for seven years after the gift and its value falls out of account for the IHT bill on death. A gift of cash is free of CGT unless it has been necessary to sell something to realise the cash.

You cannot retain any benefit in the asset gifted, so parents can't continue to receive income off it or give away their home and continue to live in it. A pre-inheritance advance is not brought back into account on the parent's death unless there is an express provision to do so in the Will, so it is necessary to decide on this and make any necessary changes to the Will.

Parents cannot keep control of their gift. If the child marries or invests in business, there is a risk that on the failure of the marriage or the business those assets will be lost to the family. On divorce, pre-nuptial agreements may not be honoured so the benefit of the gift may end up with the ex spouse.

Create a trust and keep control?

Wealthier parents could set up a trust for the benefit of their children and grandchildren.

By appointing themselves as trustees and making a gift of assets into the trust, they can keep control over the funds.

But they cannot benefit from the capital or income of the assets in the trust.

Future increases in value of the assets in the trust are kept outside the parents' estates but the transfer into the trust is a disposal for CGT, although if there is a CGT liability, payment can be deferred and payable from trust assets on eventual disposal from the trust.

A gift into trust is also subject to IHT at the date of the gift so the value of the gift should be kept beneath the IHT limit. Both parents have a nil rate band so could create a trust each. However there is also IHT every ten years, a high rate of income tax - 45% at present - and a significant administrative burden in running a trust, so advice is necessary before going down this route.

CHAPTER 14

INCOME AND PROPERTY TAX PLANNING WHEN YOUR CHILDREN LIVE WITH YOU

Children are now living with their parents for much longer than in the past. How does this impact you and your children's tax position, and crucially does it pave the way for any tax planning?

Transfer income

Whether your children are under or over the age of 18 they will be taxed independently of you. There are anti avoidance rules though that can apply when children are aged under 18. These effectively mean that you can't transfer income to minor children as it will still be taxed on you.

These provisions don't apply when your children are aged over 18.

So you can transfer investments such as property with the income then being taxed on the children. You'd need to watch out for the capital gains tax implications of any transfer, and reliefs would need to be considered.

Of course there's no requirement that your children live you, just that they're aged over 18 to stop the income being taxed on you.

House

You should still qualify for full principal private residence relief on a disposal of the property as it's occupied as your main residence.

If you're sectioning part of the house off, and for example could be building them a separate annexe to occupy you'd need to be careful.

You only qualify for the capital gains tax exemption on any part of the property that you occupy as a main residence. So if there is a part of the property occupied by other adults -- particularly if they are paying a rent you could run into problems on a future disposal of the property.

If your children are looking to live with you for the long term you could consider transferring part of the property to them. This could be particularly beneficial if they occupy part of the property such as an annexe and pay you a rent.

A transfer of a share in the property would be a disposal for CGT purposes, however as it's your main residence you'd qualify for PPR relief. Even if it's let out to a family member provided you make the transfer within 18 months of the date the letting commenced you'd qualify for full PPR relief.

Provided they own the share in the property that corresponds with their occupation on a disposal of the property in the future they would then qualify for PPR relief on their share.

Having your children living with you can be useful in terms of reducing inheritance tax as well.

For many people their main residence is their highest value asset.

Unfortunately inheritance tax planning for the family home is notoriously difficult. This is mainly due to the gift with reservation of benefit provisions.

These apply so that if you gift a share of the property but then continue to benefit from that property (eg by occupying it) it will still stay in your estate for inheritance tax purposes.

However, where children occupy a property with their parents the parents can transfer a share of that property to them without the reservation of rules applying. The caveat to this is that the children need to actually take occupation of the property and pay their fair share of the bills.

The parent would still need to survive for 7 years before the value of the share gifted is excluded from their estate, however, provided they do this they'll see the value of their estate reduce for inheritance tax purposes.

Rental

If your children are renting part of the property you'll need to assess whether it should be taxed as rental income. In most cases it wouldn't be.

Either you'd be able to argue it wasn't a payment for the rental of the property, but was just an informal payment between family members or it would fall within the lodger provisions and wouldn't be taxed.

If though there's a clear property rental element with a separate annexe and a lease to your children you'll need to pay tax on any rental profits made. This would be calculated on standard principles and you'd be able to deduct the 10% wear and tear allowance if it's let furnished.

CHAPTER 15

CASE STUDY:AVOIDING INHERITANCE TAX AND CAPITAL GAINS TAX ON PROPERTY

Making use of the available inheritance tax ('IHT') and capital gains tax reliefs is crucial in avoiding or reducing tax. Aside from looking at the IHT and CGT reliefs in isolation though what is important is to look at how they interact, and maximise the benefit of the interaction. To show you what I mean we'll look at an example.

Patrick is aged 87. He has cash investments of £350,000. He lives in a property that is owned by his Son, Peter, aged 55. The market value of the property is £200,000.

When Patrick dies he is to leave all his assets to his Son.

The nil rate is currently £325,000 which would not ordinarily cover his estate, however in this case Patrick's wife had died 12 years before. She had no assets in her own name and therefore Patrick's executors can make a claim for his wife's unused nil rate band to be transferred to him.

He'll therefore have total nil rate bands of £650,000. The cash of £350K would easily be covered by the nil rate bands.

The problem you'll have is that if Peter had purchased the property many years earlier he will be looking at substantial capital gain when he eventually sells the property.

It would be much better for all parties if the house was retained within Patrick's estate. Even with the house included there would be no inheritance tax to pay given the £650,000 IHT exemptions. By having the property retained within his estate he could then leave it to Peter who would inherit at its current market value. This would therefore eliminate the capital gain to date and Peter could sell it immediately after inheriting it free of any CGT. The net result in this situation would be a nil tax position.

How to deal with the property?

Actually how to deal with the property and have it included within Patrick's estate is though, not straightforward.

Any transfer of the property from Peter to Patrick would be a capital gain for CGT purposes with the proceeds being deemed to be the market value. So a simple transfer from Peter to Patrick wouldn't work. What you would need to look at here was where the beneficial interest lay. In particular Patrick's estate for inheritance tax purposes will include all of the assets that he was beneficially entitled to -- not just the assets he was legally entitled to.

So if you could argue that Patrick held the beneficial interest in the property whilst Peter held the legal interest, the property would be included within Patrick's estate for IHT purposes. This beneficial interest would then be left to Peter and for CGT purposes he would hold the property (strictly the beneficial interest in the property) at its probate value.

Supporting the beneficial interest

Whether you can justify the beneficial interest being held by Patrick will depend on the facts. In particular you'd be looking at issues like who pays the bills, who has control over the property and who would receive the disposal proceeds in the event of a disposal?

To clarify matters a nominee agreement or bare trust deed is usually used.

This states something along the lines of:

I, Peter, of................. hereby acknowledge and declare that I hold a legal interest in the property of X set out in the attached Schedule which is registered in my name at the above address (the "Registered Owner",Peter) and is held by me on trust to my order upon trust for the person set out in Part II of the Schedule (the

"Beneficial Owner") and I hereby agree to transfer, deal with the property/asset/shares in such manner as the Beneficial Owner may from time to time direct.

If you can establish the beneficial interest with Peter in this case you could avoid any CGT or IHT charges on the property.

CHAPTER 16

TRANSFERRING PROPERTY TO A SPOUSE TO REDUCE TAX

It's one of the most important tax breaks available and you should always think of ways of exploiting it:

Spouses can transfer property or other assets to each other without paying any capital gains tax.

Why transfer to a spouse?

The main benefits can be:

1. If you plan to sell the property and the gain won't be covered by PPR relief, having the property owned jointly allows two annual CGT exemptions to be offset. This will exempt a gain of £22,000 in 2014/2015 (assuming the annual exemptions aren't otherwise utilised).
2. If the property is generating income, this will also be split between each of you. If one spouse pays tax at the basic rate it makes sense for them to own a significant interest in the property to benefit from this lower tax rate.
3. The tax rate benefits don't just apply for income tax. Basic rate payers pay CGT at 18% rather than 28%. Therefore there can be a useful CGT advantage to holding a property with a lower earning spouse
4. For inheritance tax purposes it can allow estates to be equalised to utilise each spouses nil rate band (although this is now less of an issue now we have the transferable nil rate band).

Making the Most of Losses

The tax break for inter-spouse transfers can also be used to make the most of capital losses.

Example

Joe is married to Stevie. Joe has a property standing at a gain of £25,000 (after all reliefs). Stevie has a capital loss of £35,000 from a disposal of investments a number of years ago.

In order to eliminate his CGT charge, Joe could simply transfer the property to Stevie. Stevie could then dispose of the property and offset her old capital loss against the current year's capital gain.

Legal points

Note that this rule applies to married couples and civil partners who are living together for at least part of the tax year in question. The Civil Partnerships Act 2004 gives civil partners the same tax treatment as married couples as of 5 December 2005.

For tax purposes a husband and wife, or civil partners, are treated as 'living together' unless they are:

- Separated under a court order or separation deed, or

- Separated and circumstances point to it being permanent.

Example

Pete and Petra decide to separate in August 2012. The decree absolute is awarded in September 2014. Pete and Petra can make tax-free transfers for the whole of the 2012/2013 tax year even though they are not 'living together' from August 2012.

For the 2013/2014 tax year they will not have been living together during any part of the tax year and therefore tax-free transfers cannot be made. Instead, it is likely that Pete and Petra will be regarded as 'connected parties' and capital gains tax will be payable based on the full market value of the assets transferred.

For periods after the decree absolute is awarded, the normal CGT rules will apply.

Watch Out For Income Tax

The transfer of property to a spouse applies not only for capital gains tax purposes but for income tax and inheritance tax too.

Example

Steve is married to Steph. Steve is a basic-rate taxpayer and Steph is a higher-rate taxpayer. Steve owns a property and decides to transfer   half
of this to his wife so that two annual CGT exemptions can be utilised when the property is eventually sold.

The problem with this strategy is that if the property is ever rented , these will be taxed in Steve's and Steph's hands equally. Steve will pay 20% income tax as he is a basic-rate taxpayer, but Steph will pay tax at 40%.

HMRC Election

Where assets are held jointly by spouses the general rule is that Revenue and Customs will treat you each as being entitled to 50% of the income. This is irrespective of the actual ownership, and could work to your advantage. For example, if a higher earning spouse actually enjoys 90% of the income, he could benefit from being taxed on just 50% of the income.

If you wish to split income in any other proportion, you are permitted to submit an election to HMRC stating what proportion you each own. Therefore if you wanted to be taxed on 90% of the rental income with your wife taxed on the remaining 10%, you could make this election and HMRC would accept it. (The necessary   form   is   available   from: www.hmrc.gov.uk/forms/form17.pdf)

Note that this proportion would then usually be taken as the ownership for CGT purposes and care would need to be taken when considering whether to make the election.

Transfers and CGT

In order to minimise any adverse income tax consequences you may think it's best to simply transfer the property interest immediately prior to a disposal.

However, transferring property to a spouse to minimise CGT needs to be approached with caution. It is advisable that the final disposal does not take place just after the interspouse transfer. It is possible that anti-avoidance provisions could be invoked by HMRC.

Frequently, husband and wife transfers are made with little supporting documentation. As a minimum, a transfer of the beneficial interest should be undertaken, and in this case supporting evidence should include a signed and dated deed of gift.

For added certainty, should HMRC enquire into the matter, you may decide to amend the legal registered interest showing the joint ownership of the property.

The transfer should be a reality and not merely an artificial exercise which HMRC could argue is a 'sham'.

17. NON-RESIDENTS PURCHASING UK PROPERTY

It is useful to consider a typical scenario, where a UK non-resident and non-domiciled individual wishes to purchase a UK property.

Jack is resident and domiciled in Spain. He has relatives in the UK and is interested in purchasing a property here because (a) he wants somewhere to stay when he visits and (b) he has heard that UK property prices are set to rise.

The question is ... how from a tax perspective should he structure the purchase?

There are broadly two ways to buy the property:

- By using direct ownership, or
- Using some form of intermediary like a trust or company.

This chapter is based on the 2014/2015 tax year. We look at potential changes from April 2015 at the end of this chapter.

DIRECT OWNERSHIP

Capital Gains Tax

From a capital gains tax perspective direct ownership is potentially attractive:

- The Principal Private Residence (PPR) relief operates to exempt a gain on the disposal of an individual's main residence. Even if the property is not, in fact, Jack's main residence, he could certainly submit an election to have it treated as his main residence.

- As he is non-resident, he would not in any case be liable to UK capital gains tax on the disposal of any assets.

Inheritance Tax

The inheritance tax position is, however, not as good. The holding of property in the UK would mean that Jack has a UK estate and, as well as probate being required on his death, the house would be subject to inheritance tax to the extent that the value exceeds the £325,000 nil rate band. As the value of the property is expected to rise rapidly, this could result in a significant tax bill were he to die while still owning the asset.

There are, however, a number of methods available to Jack to reduce or eliminate any inheritance tax charge:

Use of Multiple Ownership

The property could be acquired in multiple ownership. For example, Jack, his wife and children could all own the property jointly.

Provided the individuals have no other UK assets, it is likely that each share will be below the nil rate band.

In order to avoid problems with the 'gift with reservation of benefit' legislation, it is necessary to gift cash to the family members, which they can then use to purchase their shares of the property.

The gift, with reservation of benefit (GROB) provisions, applies to property in particular, where an interest in a property is given away, yet the person gifting the interest still continues to reside in the property. For inheritance tax purposes, the whole value of the property is still regarded as included in the occupier's estate for inheritance tax purposes.

Gifting of Property

Another solution would be to gift cash to a younger member of the family who can then make the acquisition. The gift will be exempt from inheritance tax, provided the person making the gift survives seven years. The above GROB rules would not apply as the gift was a cash gift.

The UK pre-owned assets tax charge should also not be relevant if Jack is non-UK resident.

The property will then belong to the donee (the younger family member) and if the donee were to die, it would be included in his estate for inheritance tax purposes.

Mortgages

The value of an individual's estate is essentially the market value of the assets at the date of death, less any liabilities outstanding at the date of death.

It is therefore possible to effectively reduce any inheritance tax charge to zero by obtaining a substantial loan against the value of the property.

Provided the mortgage reduces the 'net value' of the property to below the nil rate band (currently £325,000), there will be no inheritance tax payable.

The mortgage funds obtained can be invested overseas and any interest return would then be exempt from UK income tax provided the interest income is not remitted to the UK.

USING A TRUST TO OWN THE PROPERTY

Capital Gains Tax

The Principal Private Residence relief is extended to situations where a beneficiary is entitled to occupy a house under the terms of a trust deed. In these circumstances, the trustees would be able to claim PPR relief when they sell the property.

In the case of a non-UK domiciliary, as the trustees are non-resident they would not, in any case, be liable to UK capital gains tax.

It would only be if the settlor of the trust (or his close family) were also a beneficiary and became UK resident that the gains of the trust could be attributed to him under the anti-avoidance provisions.

Inheritance Tax

The trust will be subject to special inheritance tax rules. One of the key implications is that it could be subject to an inheritance tax charge every 10 years starting with the date of commencement.

USING AN OFFSHORE COMPANY

The property could be owned by a non-resident company. In this case the non-domiciliary would own the shares in the company.

As the shares are non-UK property, they would be exempt from inheritance tax. The key risks are:

• The company's residence position may be closely scrutinised by the taxman, and it may be difficult to show that the central management and control is exercised outside the UK, particularly if all directors are UK resident and the asset of the company is a UK property. If HMRC is able to successfully argue that the company is UK resident, any gain on the disposal of the property would be subject to UK corporation tax and no PPR relief would be available.

• If the property is valued at more than £2Million the offshore company itself may be subject to UK CGT – we look at this shortly.

• In addition, on a disposal of the shares in the company, no capital gains tax would be payable by Jack provided he remained non-resident. If he were UK resident, he may not be charged to UK CGT provided the proceeds were retained outside the UK and he were subject to the remittance basis, as he's a non-UK domiciliary.

TAX PLANNING FOR NON-RESIDENTS OWNING UK PROPERTY INVESTMENT COMPANIES

Many individuals hold their UK properties in a UK company.

When these individuals move overseas and lose UK residence, they will often hold onto their property company.

The company has to pay UK corporation tax on any rental profits. However, the shareholder can potentially extract the remaining profits free of UK income tax/withholding tax and can always sell the shares in the company free of capital gains tax.

If the company sells the properties, however, corporation tax will have to be paid on the capital gains.

One important issue is financing the properties. This could come from either the UK or overseas.

UK financing is often preferred. The UK company would obtain a corporation tax deduction for the interest, but the shareholder could then extract the funds which could be invested overseas free of UK income tax. If the shareholder is resident in a tax haven, it may be possible to completely avoid income tax on the interest generated. This is potentially a win-win scenario with the interest being tax deductible in the UK company and reinvested overseas free of tax.

If financing is obtained from overseas the risk is that the tax deduction at source rules could apply. These can require tax to be deducted by the payer where the interest is from a UK source but the payment is made overseas. In the case of a UK company paying interest overseas, the net result is that the UK company may need to account for 20% income tax on the interest paid overseas.

The key issue is where the 'source' of the interest is. Revenue and Customs would look at a number of factors to determine whether the interest has a UK source:

• The residence of the debtor (this is usually taken to be the place where the debt will be enforced),
• The source from which interest is paid,
• Where the interest is paid, and
• The nature and location of any security for the debt.

If the loan were made to a UK company from overseas and in

respect of UK property, it would be likely that the interest would have a UK source and as such be subject to the deduction of tax at source rules. Therefore whilst it would be deductible for the UK company when calculating its taxable profits, there could be a 20% income tax liability on the interest.

The options to avoid this are limited if the interest is paid overseas. A payment to a UK bank avoids these issues.

The main option to reduce withholding tax on interest paid overseas would be to rely on a double tax treaty. These provide for an exemption or reduction in UK tax deducted at source depending on the particular agreement that the UK has with the country in question. You could therefore ensure that the deduction at source from the UK was eliminated.

Transferring Properties to an Offshore Company

Another option would be to transfer the properties to an offshore company. The main tax issue here would have to pay corporation tax on any capital gain made up to the date of transfer.

So, this strategy works best if there has only been a nominal increase in the value of the properties.
A transfer overseas could, however, shelter you from paying tax on any future gains. If the properties remain in a UK company, any increase in value will be subject to UK corporation tax at a rate of up to 21% from April 2014.

If the properties are held by a non-resident, UK tax on the gain could be avoided. The rental income would fall within the non-resident landlord scheme and an application would need to be made to receive the interest gross (without UK income tax deducted on the rental income).

Income tax (note not corporation tax) would be assessed via a self-assessment return. Any interest paid to a non-resident lender could still be claimed as a tax deduction in calculating the UK taxable profits.

Another benefit of holding the properties via a non UK company would be if the shareholder has lost UK domicile. A non UK domiciliary would be subject to UK inheritance tax on the value of the UK shares if it were not a trading company.

By contrast a non domiciliary wouldn't be subject to inheritance tax on the value of overseas shares if the UK properties were held via an offshore company.

2013 Changes

In order to tackle the so called enveloping of high value properties into companies, the Government has adopted a threefold approach:

- with effect from 21 March 2012 a new 15% rate of stamp duty land tax (SDLT) applies on purchases of UK residential properties worth over £2 million by non-natural persons;
- from 1 April 2013 an annual charge will apply to UK residential properties valued at over £2 million owned by non-natural persons; and
- from 6 April 2013 the CGT regime will be extended to gains on the disposal of UK residential property, and shares or interests in such property, by non-natural persons who are non-UK resident or UK resident.

The aim is to discourage enveloping of property and all three proposals will run in tandem.

Any new purchases of properties worth more than £2 million by an offshore company will suffer a 15% SDLT charge on the purchase. The annual charge based on value will then be payable going forward and, disposals of the property will now be subject to CGT.

Non Natural Persons

The proposals don't just apply to "offshore companies". They include all "non-natural persons" which encompasses companies, collective investment schemes and partnerships in which a non-natural person is a partner.

However, the 15% charge will not apply to the purchase of a

property by a trust even though one or more of the trustees is a company.

Annual Charge

An annual charge will come into effect on 1 April 2013 and will be payable at the start of the period of account, i.e., by 15 April of each year. It is proposed that the charge will operate on a pro rata basis so that if the property is sold during the year, a repayment of part of the charge can be claimed.

A return will be required each year for each relevant dwelling within the charge owned by the non-natural person.

The return must include information on the property:

its address, Land Registry title, details of the 'beneficial owners' of the property and their address if different from the property address.

The levels of the annual charge will be set at:

- £15,000 pa for properties valued at between £2 - 5 million;
- £35,000 for properties valued at between £5 - 10 million;
- £70,000 for properties valued at between £10 - 20 million;
- £140,000 for properties worth more than £20 million.

Introducing an annual charge on capital values means that the UK now has its first form of wealth tax (a form of tax found in many European jurisdictions including France and Spain).

In the 2014 Budget the amounts of the annual charge were increased with the lowest amount increasing to £15,400 and the highest £140,750.

New CGT charge

The new charge to capital gains tax will not apply to trustees (although they may be subject to tax under other, existing provisions). However, contrary to the Treasury's previous announcements, the charge will apply to both UK resident and non-UK resident non-natural persons.

The charge will only apply to "ATED-related gains": The ATED-related gains are essentially the gains from 6 April 2013 or the day of acquisition (if later).

If, for part of the period of ownership, the property was exempt from the Annual Charge, there is a reduction in the amount of gain subject to the capital gains tax charge to reflect this period of exemption.

In addition, where a UK resident non-natural person disposes of a property held pre-6 April 2013, the gains arising on a disposal will be split between pre-6 April 2013 gains and from 6 April 2013 gains. The gains treated as arising pre-6 April 2013 gains will be charged to corporation tax, if applicable, while gains from 6 April 2013 will be subject to capital gains tax.

A seller may elect to be charged to capital gains tax instead for the whole gain and must make an election on their tax return if they wish to do so.

ATED-related gains will not be attributed to shareholders in offshore close companies.

There are complex provisions regarding the use of any losses realised from the sale of high-value UK residential property.

In essence, losses can only be used to offset future gains arising from the sale of high-value UK residential property.

There are also provisions that deem a minimum consideration of £2 million on sale when calculating the loss available.

The rate of tax, and latent gains

The CGT charge will only apply to disposals of residential property where the amount of the consideration for the disposal exceeds £2 million.

As stated above, there is to be 'grandfathering' (i.e., protection for) latent gains that have accrued but not been realised before the extension of the CGT regime.

Although the property market as a whole has seen prices fall or remain static in recent years, those at the higher end of the market have seen large increases and substantial gains could have been built up where properties have been held for a longer period of time.

The rate of CGT will be 28%.

Meaning of 'residential property'

The definition of residential property for these purposes will follow the meaning of 'dwelling' used for the 15% SDLT rate and the new annual charge.

The CGT regime will apply to disposals of residential property in enveloped structures irrespective of the use to which it is put. For example, it will apply to commercially let residential property.

What to do if you are caught by the new anti avoidance rules?

There are a couple of options that could be considered:

De-enveloping

One option is to remove the property from the ownership of the company and move it into personal ownership.
As a result of this new legislation, many people holding such property through BVI companies are thinking about "de-enveloping".

In most cases, the de-enveloping process will be carried out by

(i) placing the BVI (or other offshore) company into voluntary liquidation and then

(ii) distributing in specie the affected property holdings.

This avoids the new punitive tax regime, but it clearly exposes the ultimate beneficial owner (if a non-dom) to UK Inheritance Tax and results in the loss of confidentiality which they previously enjoyed. CGT may also be a determining factor in whether this is a viable option. There might also be other issues if the non-dom is resident in the UK.

Offshore trust structure

For many non-doms a preferable approach may be to convert their offshore company holding structure to an offshore trust holding structure.

Corporate trustees are exempt from the above taxes and for most people transferring property already owned by an offshore company to an offshore trust may be the most cost effective way forward.

Where an offshore trust structure is already in place, with trustees holding a BVI company which in turn holds UK property, it might be advantageous to de-envelope the UK property (by liquidating the BVI company) so that the property is then held directly by the trustees.

Alternatively, if the BVI company is held directly by a non-dom, he or she may consider transferring the shares into an offshore trust now shortly before the BVI company is liquidated, with the same end result of the property then being held directly by trustees.

If the trustees are individuals, they should retire in favour of corporate trustees, so the tax exemptions can be enjoyed.

Budget 2014 changes

They will reduce the £2,000,000 threshold to £500,000.

There will now be three "bands" that can be affected by these "ATED" provisions:

- Properties valued between £500K - £1Million
- Properties valued between £1Million - £2Million

- Properties valued over £2Million

The existing reliefs and exemptions will apply.

How the new rules will apply

Properties valued between £500K - £1Million

ATED - This will apply from 1 April 2016 and there will be an annual charge of £3,500 payable by the company.

SDLT- SDLT at 15% will be paid for all properties purchased via a company above £500K on or after 20 March 2014.

CGT- The extension to the ATED-related CGT charge will take effect from 6 April 2016 and will apply only to that part of the gain that is accrued on or after that date.

Properties valued between £1Million - £2Million

ATED - This will apply from 1 April 2015 and there will be an annual charge of £7,000 payable by the company.

SDLT- SDLT at 15% will be paid for all properties purchased via a company above above £500K on or after 20 March 2014.

CGT- The extension to the ATED-related CGT charge will take effect from 6 April 2015 and will apply only to that part of the gain that is accrued on or after that date.

Properties valued above £2Million

There will be no changes to these and the existing ATED regime will apply.

HOW SHOULD YOU PURCHASE UK PROPERTY AS A NON-RESIDENT GIVEN THE 2015 CHANGES?

The proposal to charge non UK residents to UK CGT on disposal of UK residential property will have a significant impact on how such property should be purchased as from April 2015.

It is too early to make definitive decisions, however even at this stage there are quite a few issues to consider.

The key taxes to consider will be income tax, CGT, Inheritance tax and SDLT.

From an income tax perspective, however UK property is owned, income tax will be charged on UK rental profits. This will fall under the non resident landlord scheme with basic rate tax deducted at source (unless a claim is made to receive income gross).

Therefore whether property is owned personally, via a company or via a trust, UK income tax would be charged. You would need to look to other structuring aspects to reduce income tax on rental profits (eg tax efficient financing).

In terms of inheritance tax (IHT), if you are non UK domiciled you would be exempt from UK IHT on foreign assets, but UK assets would be within the scope of UK IHT. You would have the nil rate band to offset but even so the tax could be significant if the property value is substantial.

Again, if you were to hold personally, considering tax efficient financing of the property could be advisable. Debt secured on the property could reduce the value of the property in the estate and reduce any IHT liability.

You could hold via an offshore company. The advantage to this is that it would effectively convert the property value into foreign property for UK IHT purposes (as the property value would then be reflected in the share value).

For non UK domiciliaries this would then take the property value outside of their estate for UK IHT. The downside is that if the property was valued in excess of £2M there would be an annual charge under the ATED provisions. There would also be a CGT charge on disposal as well as a higher SDLT rate (potentially 15%). Note that the £2M limit is reducing to £1,000,000 from 2015 and £500,000 for 2016 for the purposes of CGT and the Annual Charge.

Currently property owned by an offshore company which is valued at less than £2M would not be subject to CGT on disposal. This is the same treatment as where property is owned by a non-resident individual.

Following the 2013 Autumn Statement this may change from April 2015.

We don't know the details and scope of the proposed changes yet but it is likely that non resident individuals holding UK residential property will be subject to CGT on a disposal. It also appears as though there will not be a £2M limit. We don't know whether it will extend to offshore companies holding UK property but would assume that it would. There are therefore still a number of aspects we aren't aware of and which would need to be considered.

In terms of the most advisable structure, it may be that whether the property is owned personally or via an offshore company, UK CGT would apply from April 2015 on a disposal. In any case for properties valued in excess of £500,000 from 2016 a CGT charge would arise. The advantage of the company is that it can avoid IHT but there would then be the ATED provisions to consider.

It may be the case that if the property is less than £500,000 using an offshore company could be beneficial to avoid UK IHT. If the property is more than £500,000 you would need to consider the IHT saving with the annual ATED cost and increased SDLT cost. It could also be attractive to considering keeping the property in individual names but looking at other strategies to reduce IHT eg purchasing in joint ownership and using debt to reduce the taxable value.

The other option is to use a trust to hold the property. An offshore trust would be subject to UK IHT on the value of UK property. It wouldn't be classed as excluded property unless an offshore company was used to hold the property which would then bring the same issues as above. Note though that using a trust would bring the UK IHT regime for discretionary trusts into play.

In particular there would be an IHT "anniversary charge" every 10 years although this is at a significantly reduced IHT rate (max 6%). There would also be an IHT charge on trust distributions. Again we don't know details yet but it is likely that the offshore trust would be subject to CGT on disposals of UK residential property after April 2015.

This could however be an attractive option if the IHT/SDLT costs of individual/company ownership aren't acceptable.

CHAPTER 18

WHICH IS THE BEST WAY FOR NON DOMS TO HOLD UK PROPERTY?

It's often asked which is the best way for non doms to hold UK property. The property is often valuable, and because it is situated in the UK it will be vulnerable to inheritance tax as even foreign domiciled individuals are liable to inheritance tax on assets situated in the UK.

A traditional answer here is to ensure that the UK property is purchased by an offshore company, particularly where the property value is less than £2M (or £500,000 after 2016), to avoid the annual tax on enveloped dwellings.

The individual then owns shares in the offshore company, which is foreign property for inheritance tax purposes and excluded from the scope of inheritance tax.

However, there are some other issues which need to be considered.

One issue would be the possibility of a charge to income tax under the benefits in kind legislation on the basis that the non dom (UK resident) is an employee who is receiving the benefit of living accommodation and is liable to income tax on the annual value in the normal way plus the supplementary benefit calculated at 4% of the cost of the property over £75,000.

The argument for HMRC is straightforward. The non dom is a person in accordance with whose instructions or directions the real directors are accustomed to act. He is therefore a shadow director; a shadow director is the same as any other director, so he is an employee and has had living accommodation provided for him by the company, which by definition is provided by reason of his employment. All the conditions are met for the benefit in kind charge to arise.

There is also the question of the company's residence.

HMRC might argue that the company is resident in the UK because of the influence of the UK-based non dom on its operations, so that the central management and control of the company would take place where the non dom is resident.

Therefore, in the event of a sale the capital gain made on the property would be fully chargeable to corporation tax. No private residence relief would be available because the property would be owned by the company and not by the individual personally.

For these reasons the non dom is likely to establish a non-resident trust to purchase the property and for the trustees to arrange for the property to be held by an offshore company under their control.

This is likely to be beneficial with both the benefit in kind and the residence arguments.

However, the resident non-dom may be protected from inheritance tax and possibly from any benefit in kind charge, but he is now exposed to a charge to capital gains tax when the property is sold.

If the company makes a gain, that gain is attributable to the trustees and is taxed on him to the extent that he has received benefits from the trust - which of course he has because he has occupied the property for many years.

The full gain might not be chargeable - it depends on the length of time for which he has occupied the property and the precise calculation of the benefit he has enjoyed from the trust property, but a substantial charge will still arise. If his family members also occupy the property, they could have part of the capital gain attributed to them as well.

Until 5 April 2008, a trust established by a foreign domiciled individual did not give rise to any capital gains attributed to the beneficiaries if it was established by a foreign domiciled settlor.

Unfortunately that exemption has been removed and the beneficiaries are liable to capital gains tax by reference to capital payments.

The non dom beneficiary can still benefit from the remittance basis so that benefits received outside the UK and not remitted to the UK are protected, but in these circumstances the benefit is received in the UK.

If the property is valued at more than £2 Million (or £500,000 from 2016), there are also additional problems from using an offshore company to hold the property, namely the Annual Tax on Enveloped Dwellings, CGT charge on disposal and 15% rate of SDLT. In many cases this will make using an offshore company unattractive for tax purposes.

Going back to the start again - why are we doing this?

The real reason is inheritance tax.

In fact, it may not be a problem at all because the non dom may simply leave the property to his spouse on his death and the full spouse exemption would be available. She could then decide what to do with the property having regard to her own tax position. In many cases, the property is sold, being too large for the widow in her new circumstances. The problem therefore disappears.

The risk though is if both spouses die in some accident and there is no spouse exemption, the full value becomes immediately chargeable.

CHAPTER 19

ADVANCED TAX PLANNING FOR NON DOMS USING OFFSHORE TRUSTS TO PURCHASE UK PROPERTY

Here's one idea for some advanced tax planning for non doms looking to remit offshore income gains into the UK free of UK tax.

Scenario:

You have a non dom with substantial unremitted income or capital gains. They want to bring cash into the UK to acquire a UK property but avoid inheritance tax.

They could of course use an offshore company but this would create problems in terms of the non dom occupying the property (as there could be benefit in kind/income tax implications with the use of the property at less than market rent).

One option to use the offshore funds to acquire a UK property directly in their own name, whilst avoiding many of the anti avoidance rules is as follows:

- They acquire shares in an offshore company containing an offshore asset.
- The shares in the offshore company are transferred to an offshore trust which has the non dom as a beneficiary for life. The transfer of the shares would be a disposal but as the non dom is claiming the remittance basis there is no CGT charge. Note that we therefore assume the non dom is paying the £30K/£50K tax charge.
- The offshore company sells the asset. This would be a disposal for CGT purposes but as the company is non resident there would be no CGT charge.

The non dom is claiming the remittance basis and paying the £30,000/£50,000 tax charge and therefore there would be no tax charge under the anti avoidance rules.

- The offshore company then loans the proceeds from the sale to the offshore trust on an arms length basis (ie interest is payable from the offshore trust to the company).
- The non dom then borrows the proceeds from the Trust interest-free and uses them to buy a house; They have charged the house to the Trust, which has charged the debt to the company;
- Each year, the Trustee waives its right to a dividend, in consideration for which the company waives its right to interest.

So you have a net position where the non dom owns the property in their own name. Although the property would fall within their UK estate for inheritance tax purposes the loan to the offshore trust would reduce the value of their estate.

On a future disposal of the property they'd be able to qualify for principal private residence relief to eliminate the capital gain.

Of course if the non dom had left the UK prior to the disposal the capital gain would be free of UK CGT in any case.

Clearly this kind of planning would only be undertaken by someone with substantial resources given you'd need to establish the various entities and ensure they were non resident as well as the other set up costs of such a structure.

As always ensure that you tax detailed advice.

20.CGT, DIVORCE AND YOUR NEW PARTNER

As we all know divorce is becoming more common. When you're looking at transferring assets the tax position should always be taken into account, and this applies equally to transfers between former spouses.

This chapter looks at tax planning for couple separating/divorcing as well as how to hold assets with new partners.

The first point to note is that a transfer of an interest in a property will be a disposal for CGT purposes.

One of the key assets for most married couples will be their main residence or other property investments.

However whether this is charged to CGT or not will depend on when the transfer is made.

Firstly there's the general rules relating to transfers between spouses. Any transfer in the tax year that you separate would be covered by the nil gain/nil loss rules. This means that irrespective of the use of the property there would be no immediate tax charge.

If you transfer after the tax year of separation these rules won't apply and you'll need to consider the use of the property and your own position to assess any CGT.

Note that it's the year of separation and not divorce that is important here. You're classed as separating in the year of permanent separation. This is defined as separating in circumstances likely to be permanent.

Therefore in most cases a transfer of title in the tax year of separation would be advisable. Of course this is frequently not possible and transfers are often made after this point as part of the divorce arrangements.

In this case you'd then need to consider any other tax reliefs that you're entitled to.

For many people they'd be looking to transfer a former residence to their partner - perhaps in exchange for other assets or a cash settlement. The capital gain would be calculated with the proceeds based on the market value in most cases.

The key relief would be principal private residence ('PPR') relief.

This provides an exemption for all or part of the capital gain where a property has been a main residence. Therefore providing you used to occupy it as a main residence you'll get a CGT exemption on the property providing you transferred it to your former spouse within 36 months of moving out. This is reducing to 18 months from 6 April 2014.

This will cover most transfers. Even if you moved out a considerable period before the transfer and have exceeded the 18 month period you could still qualify for PPR relief.

S225B TCGA 1992 allows the former matrimonial or civil partnership home to be treated as the only or main residence of the transferring spouse from the date his or her occupation ceased until the earlier of:

- the date of transfer and
- the date on which the spouse to whom the property is transferred ceases to use it as his or her main residence

This can therefore still provide for a CGT exemption on the property.

If you have acquired another property since moving out (either on a lease or as a purchase) you need to be careful. You can still qualify for the last 18 months deemed occupation on your old home without any loss of relief on your new property.

However if you opt to rely on the S225B you'll then lose PPR relief on your new property for the period that you'd deemed to occupy the 'old' property.

New property

Where you meet a new partner and look to purchase a house together this would be the main residence of both you and your new partner. Therefore if this was owned in joint names full principal private residence ('PPR') relief should be available on a future disposal.

If you and your new partner aren't married you could each have a different main residence. If therefore your new partner has another property there are a number of options available.

> You could buy the new property in joint names and retain the other property in your partners name

> You could buy the new property in your name and have the other property in your partners name

> You could have both properties in both names

For many people the second option would be preferred. As a couple you can have different main residences and therefore this could maximise the CGT relief by allowing both properties to qualify.

You would however need to ensure that each property was actually the main residence of the owner.

In order for a property to be a residence there needs to be a form of legal or equitable interest in the property as well as actual occupation of the property. Therefore if your partner owned their property only and actually occupied it on a regular basis it should be their only/main residence and qualify for PPR relief.

The property you own should not be their main residence or even a residence in this case if they held no interest in the property (and therefore the PPR election would not be necessary).

It's important though that they do still occupy their property as a residence and stay there regularly. If it was rented it would clearly not be a residence.

If both properties were in joint names your property would be fully exempt as it is likely to be you and your partners main residence. Their property would be subject to CGT, except for any PPR relief on your partners interest if it used to be her main residence.

Note that if your partner occupied your property and her own property she could submit a PPR election to nominate her property as her main residence. She would then lose your property as her main residence for the period of the nomination.

There are therefore a number of different options for structuring the ownership of properties with a new partner. If occupation can realistically be split, having two properties in separate names is a good option to maximise the PPR relief on a future disposal.

21. BENEFICIAL OWNERSHIP, RECEIVING A SHARE OF THE PROCEEDS AND REDUCING CAPITAL GAINS TAX

When looking at the capital gains tax position on the disposal of property, the beneficial interest can have a significant impact.

CGT follows primarily the beneficial, as opposed to the legal interest. So the title holder is not necessarily the one subject to CGT on the disposal. Good examples of this are bare trustees and nominees.

So if you have a case where A, is the legal owner but holds the property as a nominee or bare trustee for B, on a disposal of the property it is B that is subject to CGT. Similarly there is no CGT charge on any transfer of the legal interest from A to B.

This, or at least variations on this, are very common. There are many instances where a property is held legally by one individual but actually occupied by another. In this case unless you can show that the occupier of the property actually held the beneficial interest, any capital gain on disposal would arise to the legal owner and would be subject to CGT.

By contrast if the occupier was subject to CGT they may well qualify for a CGT exemption under the principal private residence ('PPR') relief rules.

So determining the beneficial interest can be very important for CGT purposes. It has been held in various cases that if a spouse contributes directly or indirectly towards the initial cost, or towards mortgage instalments, he/she acquires, in equity, an interest in the matrimonial home proportional to those contributions even though the other spouse alone is registered as the legal owner.

In other cases the beneficial interest will depend on who has the 'rights and responsibilities of ownership'. This will include the responsibility for bills, ability to occupy it, ability to determine when it is sold, benefiting from the proceeds of sale etc.

If you wanted to argue that property was held as a nominee or bare trustee it is usually advisable to back all this up with a nominee agreement specifically stating who holds the beneficial interest in the property.

Proceeds of sale

One point that is worth noting is that just receiving a share of the proceeds of sale would not in itself mean that a share of the beneficial interest was held. It could be argued that this was just an allocation of the proceeds and providing the recipient had no other interest or rights over the property no beneficial entitlement could arise.

This could be useful if you have a situation where A wishes to purchase a property for B. The property will be occupied by B and A still wants to benefit from the future proceeds of sale. By carefully structuring the agreement between A and B to show that A has no beneficial entitlement but can receive a share of the proceeds the gain would arise fully on B and as such would be exempt from CGT as his main residence.

Example

Jack bought a house in January 2006 for £50,000 and occupied it with his wife until January 2007, when they separated. He bought a new house for himself whilst she remained in the matrimonial home. They divorced in May 2009.

In August 2013 the Court ordered that Jill should be given 1/3 of the proceeds of sale of the matrimonial home. In January 2014 the house was sold for £180,000.

The gain accruing to Jack is computed as follows

	£
Proceeds	180,000
Less Cost	50,000

Net gain	130,000

Jacks Private residence relief

Period of ownership January 2006 - January 2014 = 8 years
Period of only or main residence:

January 2006 - January 2007 = 1 year + last 3 years = 4 years PPR
relief = 4/8 * £130,000 = £65,000

The chargeable gain is £65,000 before the annual exemption.

Jack is not entitled to a deduction for the £60,000 paid to Jill because this sum is an allocation of the proceeds and not a deduction in arriving at the gain.

Jill is not charged to Capital Gains Tax on the £60,000 she has received. It represents financial provision for her ordered by the Court and is not a sum received in consideration for the disposal of an asset.

So receiving the proceeds of sale is separate and distinct from the beneficial/equitable ownership and could be used in appropriate cases to minimise CGT on the disposal of assets.

The key issue is to ensure that the initial purchase is structured correctly with the beneficial ownership held by the individual subject to the lowest taxes eg the occupier for PPR relief purposes or an individual who will become non UK resident (eg to obtain the CGT exemption).

22.REDUCING CGT WHEN TRANSFERRING PROPERTY TO CHILDREN (INCLUDING AN EXAMPLE OF HOW TO SAVE £23,520 IN CGT)

Transferring property to children is popular for a number of reasons. In tax terms it's usually as part of an inheritance tax planning strategy. Any transfer of a property would be a potentially exempt transfer ('PET') representing the undervalue that has been transferred.

Therefore if the transfer was a gift with nothing received in return there would be a PET equivalent to the market value of the property. This would be excluded from your estate after 7 years provided you don't receive any benefit from the property. If, for example, the property was rented and you still received some of the rental income it would not drop out of your estate after 7 years. In most cases though a transfer is usually made to reduce a prospective inheritance tax charge.

The main downside with a transfer of property to children is that this will be a disposal for capital gains tax purposes.

The proceeds will be the market value of the property. For CGT purposes any agreed purchase price is ignored.

The CGT calculation is very straightforward.

Effectively it'll be the difference between the market value of the property and the original cost. Any gain is then taxed at 18% or 28%.

How to reduce the CGT charge

Some of the options to reduce the CGT charge include:

> •Ensure you claim all deductions. You can claim for not

only the costs of buying and selling the property (including stamp duty) but also for any 'enhancement expenditure'.

Enhancement expenditure includes any capital expenditure on the property that is reflected in it when it is sold. The types of things this will include are new kitchens, bathrooms, conservatory, rewiring, new plumbing, new lights etc

•Make the most of the CGT annual exemption

If you own the property solely in your name you should consider a transfer of an interest in the property to your spouse before transferring to your children. Provided they have not used their annual CGT exemption for the tax year you'll be able to double the annual exemptions on the disposal and exempt around £22,000 of the gain from CGT.

You could also consider spreading the disposal over the course of a number of tax years.

You could therefore transfer 25% of the property per year to your children over a 4 year period. This would ensure that only 25% of the gain was charged on you each year. If you also owned it with your spouse you'd be looking at a substantial CGT saving thanks to the annual CGT exemption. The annual exemptions would cover £84,000 of any gain which represents a CGT saving of £23,520.

•Invest in EIS shares

By investing in EIS shares you can defer the gain that arises. You would though need to make a separate investment equivalent to the capital gain that is realised.

•Uplift in base cost

Don't forget that if you owned the property before March 1982 you can swap your acquisition cost for the market value when calculating the capital gain.

In most cases this will reduce your capital gain

•Principal Private Residence relief

This will be a significant relief for many. If you've occupied the property as your main residence you'll be able to claim Principal Private Residence relief on the disposal.

This reduces the capital gain based on the formula:

Period of occupation as a main residence/Period of ownership

In all cases where you've occupied it at some point the last 36 months is deemed occupation (reducing to 18 months after April 2014).

•Lettings relief

If you've occupied it as a main residence at any point (even for a small period) you can claim lettings relief. This reduces the gain for the lower of:

– Amount of PPR relief
– £40,000
– Gain attributable to the letting

The combination of PPR relief and Lettings relief can be very effective in reducing CGT

•Non residency

If you're non UK resident you can transfer the property to your kids free of CGT. Note though that if you're a short term non resident you'll need to remain non resident for 6 tax years to stop the gain being charged in the tax year of your return.

23. SHOULD YOU SELL OR LET YOUR FORMER HOME?

In the past when you wanted to buy a new house you simply sold the old one. Now, its not that simple and many people are looking to retain their former house, either for financial reasons (so they can benefit from a rising property market) or personal reasons (in that they may wish to occupy the property again).

There are a number of factors that will need to be considered when weighing up whether you should simply sell the property or retain it, however how you'll be taxed may be crucial.

As well as if you should sell the property, a related question is when you should sell the property. For example it's common to keep a property and let it out for a few years after you've bought your new one. But in tax terms is there a definite time that you should sell this - or does it not matter if you just carry on renting it out right up until you decide to sell it?

Capital gains tax ('CGT')

If you sold the property, after you moved out principal private residence ('PPR') relief would cover any gain arising in full. If you decided to let the property for a number of years before disposal you may be liable to capital gains tax on the disposal dependent on the number of years absence and the gain arising.

As we've seen, as from April 2014 the last 18 months of ownership would always be deemed to be occupied by you irrespective of the use of the property during this period.

There are also more 'deemed periods of occupation' that you could be entitled to although the qualifying conditions for these are much stricter.

If you go overseas under a contract of employment, occupy the property as a main residence both before and after your period of absence, and have no other residence overseas, the entire period of absence overseas would be deemed occupation. The main time this would be likely to apply would be where you worked overseas and lived in employer provided accommodation.

If the property was let you wouldn't then be able to establish the property as your main residence for this period. However, Lettings Relief would then apply.

Therefore the position in terms of timing would be:

- If you were to sell the property within 18 months of ceasing to occupy it any gain arising would be fully covered by PPR relief.
- If you left it for more than 18 months but did not let it out, you'd qualify for partial PPR relief that would eliminate part of the remaining gain.
- If you left it for more than 18 months but did let it out you'd qualify for partial PPR relief and lettings relief which would reduce and may well eliminate the remaining gain.

You should also bear in mind that you would be able to claim the annual CGT exemption which could eliminate any small gain remaining.

Capital loss

In the unfortunate event that you sold the property at a loss, a loss on a main residence would not be an allowable capital loss and therefore couldn't be offset against income or gains.

Rate of CGT

The rate of CGT is now 18% or 28% depending on your other income.

Rental income

If you decide to rent the property out you will be subject to income tax on the rental 'profit'.

When calculating the rental profit, you are permitted to deduct any expenses incurred 'wholly and exclusively' for the purpose of the letting business. Under tax law, you are regarded as carrying on a business of letting properties.

Therefore typical expenses that you will obtain a deduction for are:

- Repairs to the let property
- Insurance
- Any utility bills
- Interest on a loan/mortgage used for the property.

Note its only the interest on the mortgage that would be an allowable expense -and not the full capital repayment element of the payment.

If you incurred a rental loss this would be offset against any future rental profits arising.

Furnished v Unfurnished

There are few differences from a tax perspective whether a property is let furnished or unfurnished. The main one is that a furnished property would be entitled to the wear and tear allowance. This is a 10% reduction in the net rental income, and this could therefore result in a lower income tax charge.

Transfer to a company

A common question is whether a transfer to a company will yield any benefits.

The transfer to a UK company would realise a gain although this would be fully covered by PPR relief. On a future disposal by the company any uplift in the value of the property would be taxed in the UK company even if the disposal was only in 12 months time.

You could retain ownership of the property but simply use the company just in a management capacity. This would enable some of the rent to effectively be diverted to the UK company, to be taxed at 20%. The tax saving would however be marginal unless you planned to retain the funds within the company (we have covered the use of a property service company in a separate article).

You could consider using an offshore company, however this would not offer any real advantages unless the company was controlled from overseas. If it was controlled in the UK, it would be UK resident and as such fully charged to UK corporation tax just as for a UK company.

If you could establish an overseas controlled company that traded overseas, this could be beneficial to divert part of the rental income into a tax free entity.

The main problem in using a company would be that as from 2016 many properties valued at more than £500,000 and held in a company will be subject to an annual tax charge of £3,500. In addition SDLT would be charged at 15% on purchase.

Emigration

You could also consider emigrating overseas. You would still be liable to UK income tax on the rental income, however providing your absence overseas was for at least six complete tax years you would not be liable to UK CGT on a disposal of the property.

24. SHOULD YOU REOCCUPY A PROPERTY PRIOR TO SELLING IT?

If you have a property that has been occupied as a main residence by you at any time in your period of ownership you'll be able to claim principal private residence ('PPR') relief on the disposal.

This will then reduce the amount of CGT that you pay. PPR relief is given based on the following:

Period of occupation/Period of ownership

So if you occupy it for 5 years and you've owned it for 10 you'll get 50% PPR relief.

However when taking into account the period of occupation you are always deemed to have occupied it for the last 18 months of ownership (providing it was your main residence at some other point in your ownership).

Therefore if you purchased it in 2004 and sold it in 2014 you've have owned it for 10 years. If you occupied it between 2001 - 2004 you'd have 3 years of actual occupation and also have the 18 months deemed occupation (total 4.5 years and therefore 45% PPR relief in this case).

If you occupied it between January 2013 – June 2014 you'd have 18 months occupation. Why? Well because the last 18 months deemed ownership would cover the period of actual occupation in any case.

So based on this in many cases there would be no benefit to be gained by reoccupying a property before disposal - as you're already deemed to be occupying it.

Of course if you've never previously occupied the property as a main residence it may be advantageous to occupy it as a main residence before disposal (eg for 6-12 months) as this would then entitle you to the last 18 months of deemed occupation. This would therefore increase your amount of PPR relief (and therefore lower your CGT).

Other deemed periods

There is however another case where it can be very beneficial to reoccupy a property prior to the disposal.

Where you work overseas (or in certain other special cases eg if you work away in the UK) you can be deemed to have occupied the property for your period of absence (even if it's rented) providing:

- You have no other residence overseas, and
- You occupy the property both before and after the period of absence.

So if you have no other residence (which means no other freehold or leasehold property eg employer provided accommodation) you may want to look to reoccupy a property before the disposal. This could then ensure that the period of your absence was completely exempt from CGT.

The periods that qualify for this special treatment are:

- Any period when working abroad
- Up to 4 years if working away in the UK
- Up to 3 years for any other purpose

25. WHEN A PROPERTY CAN BE YOUR MAIN RESIDENCE WITHOUT YOU OCCUPYING IT

As we've seen in previous chapters, ensuring that a property is your main residence can be very advantageous for the purposes of capital gains tax. In particular a main residence will qualify for either a full or partial CGT exemption.

Usually in order to claim a property as a main residence it is a prerequisite that it has been occupied as a residence.

There are two main ways of making a property a main residence.

Firstly, you could actually occupy it as your main home, or Secondly, you could occupy it along with another property and make a PPR election for one of the properties to be the main residence for CGT purposes.

Whichever way you go though you need to occupy it as a residence first.

There are no hard and fast rules as to how long to occupy the property before it can be classed as a residence. Some commentators suggest occupying a property for a period of 12 months, although there is no fixed period set by the Revenue and they frequently refer to the 'quality' as opposed to the 'quantity' of the occupation. It is important to ensure that the residence is genuine. For example the property should be your registered address for the electoral register, and your employers should be informed of the new address.

If you've not actually occupied a property though you won't be able to establish it as a residence and there won't be any principal private residence ('PPR') relief. It doesn't matter whether you bought it with the intention of occupying it as a residence or not.

The exception

There is however an exception this which will apply where you can make a property a residence even though you haven't actually occupied it. In this case it will depend crucially on your intention as to your future occupation and not what you actually do.

The exception is for anyone who lives in job related accommodation. In this case they can purchase another property and this will be their residence providing they intend to occupy it as their main residence at some point in the future.

It's important to note that even if the property is never actually occupied as a main residence it can still be entitled to principal private residence relief. The Revenue manuals make it clear that:

'...It may be that the individual never in fact occupies the relevant dwelling house because of a change in circumstances or for some other reason. Provided it was always the individuals intention to occupy the relevant dwelling house, relief will be available...'

Therefore provided there is the intention to occupy it will be a residence for CGT purposes. This will even be the case if the property is let out whilst you are living in the job related accommodation.

What is job related accommodation?

The bad news is that job related accommodation is construed very strictly. In particular it will only apply where accommodation is provided that is:

- necessary for the proper performance of the duties
- provided for the better performance of the duties and the employment is one of the kinds in which it is customary for employers to provide living accommodation
- required as part of arrangements for a special security threat

In most cases, it will be a case of seeing if either of the first two apply.

Different classes of job related accommodation

The types of people that will generally qualify under the job related accommodation exception include:

- agricultural workers who live on farms or agricultural estates.
- lock-gate and level-crossing gate keepers
- caretakers living on the premises.
- stewards and green keepers living on the premises
- managers of public houses living on the premises
- wardens of sheltered housing schemes living on the premises where they are on call outside normal working hours
- police officers
- Ministry of Defence police
- prison governors, officers and chaplains
- clergymen and ministers of religion unless engaged on purely administrative duties
- pre-registration house officers
- members of HM Forces
- members of the Diplomatic Service
- managers of newsagent shops that have paper rounds,
- managers of traditional off-licence shops, that is those with opening hours broadly equivalent to those of a public house,
- in boarding schools where staff are provided with accommodation on or near the school premises
- head teacher
- other teachers with pastoral or other irregular contractual responsibilities outside normal school hours (for example house masters)
- bursar
- matron, nurse and doctor

If you are provided accommodation that is job related you can then purchase another property, intend to live in it and potentially sell it free of CGT in the future.

Even if you are provided job related accommodation you'll need to consider what type of accommodation it is, as this will have an important impact on the relief claimed.

Broadly speaking you could be provided accommodation either under a tenancy (eg a lease) or under a licence.

If it's a licence (eg employer owned and provided accommodation with no ownership rights by you) you will have no interest in the job related accommodation and your only residence will be the property that you actually own and intend to occupy in the future.

If, however, you occupy it under a lease or tenancy your job related accommodation will itself be a residence for you.

This is important as it means you have two residences and to get the CGT exemption on the property that you own you'll then need to make a PPR election in favour of this property (effectively by writing a letter to the revenue outlining the details of the two properties along with which one you want to treat as your main residence).

ABOUT THE AUTHOR

Lee Hadnum LLB ACA CTA is a UK tax specialist. He is a Chartered Accountant and Chartered Tax Adviser and is the Editor of the popular tax planning website:

www.wealthprotectionreport.co.uk

Lee is also the author of a number of best selling tax planning books.

OTHER TAX GUIDES

- **Tax Planning Techniques Of The Rich & Famous** - Essential reading for anyone who wants to use the same tax planning techniques as the most successful Entrepreneurs, large corporations and celebrities

- **The Worlds Best Tax Havens 2014/2015** – 220 page book looking at the worlds best offshore jurisdictions in detail

- **Non Resident & Offshore Tax Planning 2014/2015**– Offshore tax planning for UK residents or anyone looking to purchase UK property or trade in the UK. A comprehensive guide.

- **Tax Planning With Offshore Companies & Trusts: The A-Z Guide** - Detailed analysis of when and how you can use offshore companies and trusts to reduce your UK taxes

- **Tax Planning For Company Owners** – How company owners can reduce income tax, corporation tax and NICs

- **How To Avoid CGT In 2013/2014** – Tax planning for anyone looking to reduce UK capital gains tax

- **Buy To Let Tax Planning** – How property investors can reduce income tax, CGT and inheritance tax

- **Asset Protection Handbook** – Looks at strategies to ringfence your assets in today's increasing litigious climate

- **Working Overseas Guide** – Comprehensive analysis of how you can save tax when working overseas

- **Double Tax Treaty Planning** – How you can use double tax treaties to reduce UK taxes

DEC. 0 7 2015

Made in the USA
San Bernardino, CA
20 May 2015